Special Educational Needs for Newly Qualified and Student Teachers

A Practical Guide **Rita Cheminais**

edited by Charles Gains

 **David Fulton** Publishers

David Fulton Publishers Ltd
The Chiswick Centre, 414 Chiswick High Road, London W4 5TF

www.fultonpublishers.co.uk
www.onestopeducation.co.uk

First published in Great Britain by David Fulton Publishers 2000

David Fulton Publishers is a division of Granada Learning Limited,
part of ITV plc

British Library Cataloguing in Publication Data
A catalogue record for this book is available from the British Library.

ISBN 1 85346 707 3

Acknowledgement

In this book extracts have been used from: the *Code of Practice on the
Identification and Assessment of Special Needs*; *Excellence for All
Children: Meeting Special Educational Needs*; *Meeting Special
Educational Needs: A Programme of Action*; DfEE Circular 4/98,
Teaching: High Status, High Standards; DfEE Circular 5/99, *The
Induction Period for Newly Qualified Teachers*; *The National Curriculum:
Handbooks for Primary Teachers and Secondary Teachers in England*; and
DfEE Circular 10/99, *Social Inclusion: Pupil Support*.

Typeset by Kate Williams, Abergavenny.
Printed in Great Britain

Contents

Acknowledgements

My interest in newly qualified teachers (NQTs) and initial teacher training (ITT) students special educational needs (SEN) training has developed over the past three years. I am grateful to Paul Rafferty, Senior Lecturer in Education at Liverpool Hope University College, for giving me my first opportunity to participate in the SEN training of postgraduate certificate of education (PGCE) students.

In preparing this book I sought the opinions of the NQTs in Tameside schools. I am appreciative of the aspects of SEN that they identified as being areas of concern to them during their first year of teaching.

I am deeply indebted to my colleague Maggie Donnellan, General Adviser for Literacy in Tameside, for giving me the opportunity to coordinate the NQT Induction Programme. Ian Smith, Head of Standards and Effectiveness in Tameside, has also been a tower of strength in supporting and encouraging me in my work with NQTs.

I would like to thank Linda Devlin, and Angela Harnett from the Institute of Education at Manchester Metropolitan University, for their continued commitment and joint partnership in supporting me in my NQT role.

I am grateful to Charles Gains for his constructive comments, valued experience and informed feedback when reading the draft copies of the sections of this book.

Finally, my thanks go to my mother for her forbearance during the writing of this book.

While every effort has been made to acknowledge sources throughout the book, such is the range of SEN subjects covered, however, that I may have unintentionally omitted to mention their origin. If so, I offer my apologies to all concerned.

SEN Abbreviations

ADD	Attention Deficit Disorder
ADHD	Attention Deficit Hyperactivity Disorder
ASD	Autistic Spectrum Disorder
BDA	British Dyslexia Association
BECTA	British Educational Communications and Technology Agency
CATs	Cognitive Ability Tests
COP	Code of Practice
EAL	English as an Additional Language
EBD	Emotional and Behavioural Difficulties
EDP	Education Development Plan
EP	Educational Psychologist
EPS	Educational Psychology Service
EWO	Education Welfare Officer
GLD	Global Learning Difficulties/General Learning Difficulties
HI	Hearing Impairment
IEP	Individual Education Plan
IQ	Intelligence Quotient
LSA	Learning Support Assistant
LSS	Learning Support Service
MLD	Moderate Learning Difficulties
PMLD	Profound and Multiple Learning Difficulties
PPO	Parent Partnership Officer
PRU	Pupil Referral Unit
PS	Partially Sighted
PSP	Pastoral Support Programme
SEMERC	Special Education Microelectronic Resource Centres
SEN	Special Educational Needs
SENCO	Special Educational Needs Coordinator
SENT	Special Educational Needs Tribunal
SLD	Severe Learning Difficulties
SLT	Speech and Language Therapist
SpLD	Specific Learning Difficulties
SSA	Special Support Assistant
SSS	Sensory Support Service
VI	Visual Impairment

Introduction

What are special educational needs?

The law says that a child has special educational needs if he or
she has: *a learning difficulty* (i.e. a significantly greater difficulty
in learning than the majority of children of the same age, or
a disability which makes it difficult to use the educational
facilities generally provided locally); and if that learning
difficulty calls for: *special educational provision* (i.e. provision
additional to, or different from, that made generally for children
of the same age in local schools).
(Department for Education and Employment (DfEE) 1997b: 1.2)

What are severe and/or complex needs?

Pupils with severe and/or complex needs will include, for
example, those with autistic spectrum disorders, those with
physical and sensory disabilities, those with acute emotional
and behavioural difficulties, those with severe and profound
learning difficulties, those with specific learning difficulties, and
those with speech, language and communication difficulties.
(Teacher Training Agency (TTA) 1999: 12b)

A child is disabled if they have a physical or mental disability
that has a substantial, adverse and long-term effect on his or
her ability to carry out normal day-to-day activities. Physical
or mental disability includes sensory impairments. Hidden
disabilities are also included, e.g. mental illness or mental
health problems, learning difficulties, dyslexia, and conditions
such as diabetes or epilepsy, and those with severe disfigure-
ments.
(SEN and Disability Act 2001, Chapter 10, Part 1, Section 1)

The aim of this publication

The aim of this publication is to enable all those venturing on a teaching career to understand:
- their responsibilities under the SEN Code of Practice
- the importance of identifying pupils with SEN
- how to meet a diversity of pupils' learning and behavioural difficulties more effectively in an inclusive school, by differentiating teaching practice appropriately
- the importance of collaborative working practices with other teachers, learning support assistants (LSAs) and parents, to maximise pupil potential.

The publication will be of interest to:
- ITT students
- NQTs
- teachers returning to the profession after a career break
- those involved in training teachers
- induction tutors in schools
- SEN Coordinators (SENCOs)
- SEN Link Governors
- Local education authority (LEA) advisers responsible for SEN, and NQTs.

The format is designed to:
- act as a quick reference guide to ITT students and NQTs
- be part of a training programme – each page is complete and self-contained and can be photocopied for training purposes.

This publication is designed to be used in conjunction with the SEN Code of Practice.

Part 1

Legal Requirements and Recommendations

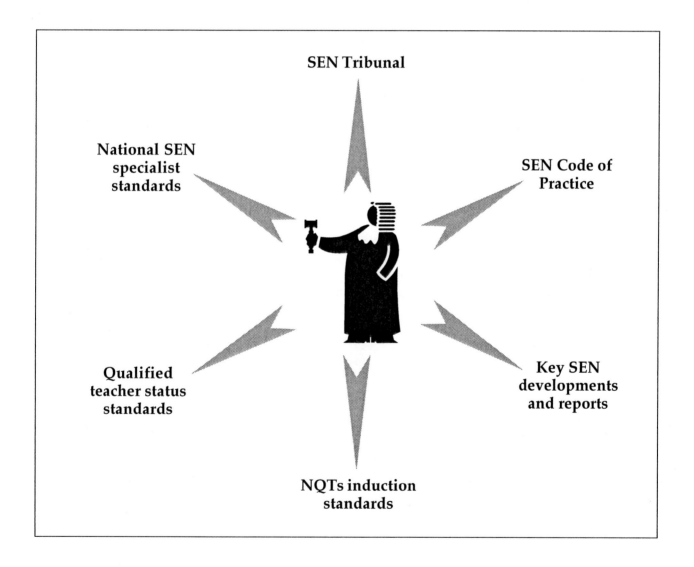

QTS and NQT Induction Standards and SEN

Training in special educational needs is a priority, whether teachers work in mainstream or special schools or in LEA support services. (DfEE 1997b, 6:5)

The professional standards to be established for the new induction year seek to ensure that all new teachers are able to identify and plan effectively to meet the needs of pupils with SEN, and to work effectively with parents and with support staff in classrooms. (DfEE 1998b, 4:2)

from . . . QTS STANDARDS	from . . . NQT INDUCTION STANDARDS
B. Planning, Teaching and Class Management **4. Planning** a. plan their teaching to achieve progression in pupils learning through: . . . v. identifying pupils who: – have special educational needs, including specific learning difficulties; – are very able; – are not yet fluent in English; and knowing where to get help in order to give positive and targeted support . . . **Teaching and Class Management** l. are familiar with the Code of Practice on the identification and assessment of special educational needs and, as part of their responsibilities under the Code, implement and keep records on [individual education plans] IEPs for pupils at Stage 2 of the Code and above . . . **D. Other Professional Requirements** d. are committed to ensuring that every pupil is given the opportunity to achieve their potential and meet the high expectations set for them . . . (DfEE 1998a: Annex A)	**Planning, Teaching and Class Management** a. sets clear targets for improvement of pupils' achievement, monitors pupils' progress towards targets and uses appropriate teaching strategies in the light of this, including, where appropriate, in relation to literacy, numeracy and other school targets; b. plans effectively to ensure that pupils have the opportunity to meet their potential, notwithstanding differences of race and gender, and taking account of the needs of pupils who are: – underachieving; – very able; – not yet fluent in English; making use of relevant information and specialist help where available; c. secures a good standard of pupil behaviour in the classroom through establishing appropriate rules and high expectations of discipline which pupils respect, acting to pre-empt and deal with inappropriate behaviour in the context of the behaviour policy of the school; d. plans effectively, where applicable, to meet the needs of pupils with special educational needs and, in collaboration with the [special educational needs coordinator] SENCO, makes an appropriate contribution to the preparation, implementation, monitoring and review of IEPs; e. takes account of ethnic and cultural diversity to enrich the curriculum and raise achievement . . . **Other Professional Requirements** h. where applicable, deploys support staff and other adults effectively in the classroom, involving them, where appropriate, in the planning and management of pupils' learning; . . . (DfEE 1999a: Annex A)

1978 Warnock Report Recommended the end of SEN categorisation; right of all children to be educated; parents as partners.

1981 Education Act (effective in Education Act 1983) Categorisation of SEN gone; SEN pupils to be educated in ordinary schools; LEAs to maintain a statement of SEN; SEN defined.

1988 Education Reform Act (Sections 17, 18, 19) related to SEN and the curriculum: modification of the curriculum, disapplication from National Curriculum, SATs introduced. Grant maintained status introduced; local management of schools (LMS) and open competition between schools for pupils.

1989 Childrens Act Related to care, upbringing and welfare of children; supervision orders. Covered children with SEN and 'looked after children'.

1992 Parents Charter (Children with Special Needs) Defined SEN, explained the assessment and statementing procedures.

1993 Education Act (Part III) Updated Education Act 1981. Introduced SEN Tribunal (SENT), pupil referral units (PRUs), and the concept of a Code of Practice for SEN. Schools to report annually to parents on SEN policy and provision.

1994 Code of Practice on the Identification and Assessment of Special Educational Needs Provided a framework for SEN policy, practice and provision. Schools and LEAs were to have regard to the recommendations made. Six sections to the SEN Code of Practice:

Section 1 – covered integration, early intervention, partnership, continuum of needs and provision; full access to the National Curriculum; mainstream provision where practicable.
Section 2 – sets out definitions, responsibilities and explains the school-based Stages 1–3.
Section 3 – Procedures explained for statutory assessment of SEN.
Section 4 – Statementing explained.
Section 5 – Assessments and statementing for children under-5.
Section 6 – Annual review of statements and transitional reviews 14–16 explained.

1995 Disability Discrimination Act (Part IV) Schools to report on the arrangements for admitting disabled pupils; schools to indicate the steps taken to prevent disabled pupils from being discriminated against; facilities available to assist school access for disabled pupils. Disabled pupils to have the right to quality education free from discrimination and segregation.

1996 Education Act (Part 4 related to SEN) Updated January 1999. Relates to pupils with learning difficulties. Outlined the duty to include SEN pupils in mainstream schools. Clarified the staged

Key SEN Developments Post-Warnock

approach of the SEN Code of Practice. Explained statutory assessment, the statementing process and the appeals procedure for the SEN Tribunal. The LEA has 6 weeks in which to decide whether to make a statutory assessment. The LEA has 10 weeks in which to carry out the assessment. The LEA decides over 10 weeks whether to issue a statement of SEN and within 2 weeks must inform parents of their decision. Parents receive a proposed statement and they have 15 days in which to decide if it is appropriate and acceptable. If not, a further 15 days to make comments are available.

Key SEN Reports

1997 *The SENCO Guide* **(DfEE 1997a)**   Covered: good practice for SENCOs; IEPs; and developing SEN policies in schools. Provided guidance to schools on the SENCO's roles and responsibilities, and how to manage and administer the SEN Code of Practice more effectively.

1997 *Excellence for All Children. Meeting Special Educational Needs* **(DfEE 1997b)**   The DfEE Green Paper on SEN covered six main themes: (i) higher expectations for SEN pupils; (ii) supporting parent partnership and strengthening parents of SEN pupils rights; (iii) increased inclusion opportunities in mainstream schools; (iv) focus on shifting from procedures to practical support for SEN; (v) training and professional development in SEN for teachers, trainee teachers and NQTs – with more multi-agency partnership between health, education and social services encouraged; (vi) promoting partnership in SEN locally, regionally and nationally.

1998 *Meeting Special Educational Needs. A Programme of Action* **(DfEE 1998b)**   Builds on the Green Paper. The aim is to improve standards and achievement in SEN. Five themes are featured: (i) working with parents – early identification, early years; (ii) improving the SEN framework – revised SEN Code of Practice, improving IEPs and standards for SENCOs; (iii) developing a more inclusive education system; (iv) developing knowledge and skills of SEN among teachers, LSAs, Educational Psychologists (EPs) and school governors; (v) working in partnership to meet SEN – regional coordination of SEN provision, improved multi-agency working, and reviewing the work of therapy services, improving post-16 provision for SEN students.

1998 *Supporting the Target Setting Process. Guidance for Effective Target Setting for Pupils with Special Educational Needs* **(DfEE 1998c)**   Differentiated performance criteria devised by the DfEE and the Qualifications and Curriculum Authority (QCA), for SEN pupils operating below National Curriculum Level 1('P' level) and within National Curriculum Levels 1 and 2 (smaller steps 1C, 1B, 1A, 2C, 2B, 2A). The criteria cover language and literacy, mathematics and personal and social development. They provide a common assessment framework which can be used at the end of an academic year or key stage. They also enable SEN pupils' achievements to be recognised and are an alternative to 'W', working towards, and disapplication.

1998 *National Standards for Special Educational Needs Coordinators* **(Teacher Training Agency (TTA) 1998)** The TTA set out the skills, knowledge, understanding, attributes, and expertise that SENCOs need to coordinate SEN provision in schools. The standards provide a framework for targeted professional training in SEN for SENCOs. Leadership and management skills are highlighted for SENCOs performing their role effectively.

1999 *National Special Educational Needs Specialist Standards* **(TTA 1999)** TTA recommend this document being used as an audit tool to help head teachers and teachers to identify their specific training and development needs in relation to effective teaching of SEN pupils with severe and complex needs. (This refers to pupils with autistic spectrum disorders, physical and sensory disabilities, emotional and behavioural difficulties (EBD), severe/profound learning difficulties, specific learning difficulties and speech, language and communication difficulties.) The standards are in two parts: the Core Standards, for all teachers, relate to effective teaching and improved curriculum access, and focus on behaviour, social and emotional development, identification, assessment, planning and basic skills; the Extension Standards relate to additional specialist knowledge required by some teachers to meet more complex and severe SEN.

1999 *Social Inclusion* **(Circulars 10/99 (DfEE 1999d) & 11/99 (DfEE 1999e))** These circulars focus on improving attendance and behaviour, reducing exclusions/disaffection and greater curriculum flexibility, and describe Pastoral Support Programmes.

1999 *From Exclusion to Inclusion. A Report of the Disability Rights Task Force* **(DfEE 1999f)** Chapter 4 relates to education and emphasises strengthening mainstream inclusion for disabled children and young people. The report recommends strengthening parental rights of children with SEN. It wants to see LEA and school policies, practice and procedures adjusted to avoid discrimination on the grounds of disability. Accessibility to schools and the curriculum must be increased.

The SEN Code of Practice

> New requirements for initial teacher training courses, ... will ensure that all newly qualified teachers understand their responsibilities under the SEN Code of Practice, are capable of identifying children with SEN, and when appropriately supported, are able to differentiate teaching practice.   (DfEE 1998b: para. 4:2)

The original SEN Code of Practice (DfEE 1994a) outlined the role and responsibility of the class teacher or form/year tutor in relation to SEN:

- identifies a child's special educational needs
- consults the child's parents and the child
- informs the SEN Coordinator, who registers the child's special educational needs
- collects relevant information about the child, consulting the SEN Coordinator
- works closely with the child in the normal classroom context
- monitors and reviews the child's progress.

(DfEE 1994a: para. 2:65)

and:

- gather information about the child and make an initial assessment of the child's special educational needs
- provide special help within the normal curriculum framework, exploring ways in which increased differentiation of classroom work might better meet the needs of the individual child.   (DfEE 1994a: paragraph 2:73)

The revised draft SEN Code of Practice, due out late 2001, is more concise than the 1994 version. There will be a family of documents accompanying the revised Code: guidance on thresholds of placement and provision; a good practice guide, and an expanded parents guide. The final version of the revised SEN Code of Practice becomes effective at the start of the academic year 2001–2002. Stage 1 is likely to disappear and *School Action* will combine Stages 1 and 2. *School Action Plus* will replace Stage 3, but will still involve external intervention. Both necessitate IEPs being put in place at school level. The SENCO's role continues to be paramount, with enough non-contact time allocated, in order to enable them to manage the SEN Code of Practice more effectively. Inclusion remains a central theme throughout the revised draft SEN Code of Practice, with well organised classrooms being the essential ingredient necessary to enable class/subject teachers to meet the needs of SEN pupils effectively. Within the inclusion agenda, the child's own views about their special educational needs are to be taken into consideration. Parent partnership arrangements continue to be important, and conciliation via a Parent Partnership Officer, independent of the LEA, will play a major role. LEAs need to make SEN funding arrangements clearer to schools, and take a greater role in monitoring how schools use the resources allocated.

> Are familiar with the Code of Practice on the identification and assessment of special educational needs
> (QTS Standards; DfEE 1998a: Annex A:4.1)

Quick Guide to the Revised Draft SEN Code of Practice

SCHOOL ACTION	SCHOOL ACTION PLUS
School takes responsibility at School Action. Amalgamation of Stages 1 & 2. Pupils are placed on the SEN Register. Increased curriculum differentiation. Some in-class support provided. IEPs in place with subject specific and cross-curricular targets. Class/subject teachers support IEP implementation within the classroom. SENCO responsible for planning, monitoring and reviewing SEN provision and pupil progress. Termly reviews of progress are advisable. Pupil can move off School Action if, after two IEP reviews, progress has been satisfactory or good.	School responsibility with support from external agencies. Replaces Stage 3. Pupil placed at School Action Plus on the SEN Register. Pupil moves to School Action Plus, if, after two reviews at School Action, little if any progress or improvement has been made. A new IEP is devised in conjunction with external agencies. Class/subject teachers support the implementation of IEPs within class. SENCO takes the lead in coordinating provision, monitoring and reviewing progress in collaboration with external agencies. If there has been an improvement, the pupil may revert back to School Action, or be removed from the SEN Register. If, after two School Action Plus reviews, progress is less than satisfactory or has deteriorated, the school, in negotiation with parents can request the LEA to make a statutory assessment. EP involvement at School Action Plus is related to assessment, and/or targeted direct intervention.
STATUTORY ASSESSMENT	**STATEMENT OF SEN**
Parents and the school can request the LEA to undertake a statutory assessment on a child identified with SEN. The LEA has six weeks to consider whether a statutory assessment should be done. The LEA has ten weeks to undertake a statutory assessment of SEN. The LEA will request reports and assessments from: head teachers, medical, psychological and social services staff, as well as from parents/carers, and the child's own perceptions. Following the outcome of statutory assessment, the LEA has two weeks in which to notify the parents of their decision: i.e. not to issue a statement of SEN with reasons; or, issue a note in lieu in place of a statement, recommending the appropriate SEN provision for a child not deemed to have severe and complex needs; or, draft a proposed statement of SEN. (The whole assessment and statementing process takes 26 weeks.)	A statement of SEN is given by the LEA when a mainstream school is unable to meet a child's severe and complex needs, from its existing resources. Parents receive a draft proposed statement. Eight weeks is given for the statement to be finalised. A statement is a legal document that specifies: the nature of the child's SEN; the necessary SEN provision from the LEA and the school; the objectives to be met; the arrangements for monitoring the child's progress; the type of school; non-educational needs (health/social services); and non-educational provision, e.g. transport, specialist aids, speech and language therapy. A statement of SEN is reviewed annually by the LEA. A statement of SEN can be amended, or cease to be maintained.

The SEN Tribunal

The Tribunal is the final arbiter in disputes between parents and LEAs. Its overriding aim is to consider the needs of the child. Each appeal is heard by a panel of three – a legally trained chairman, and two members with expertise in SEN and/or local government.   (DfEE 1997b: para. 2.14)

SENT originated from the Education Act 1993, and its regulatory powers were outlined in the Education Act 1996, Part IV. The SENT Regulations have since been amended and come into force on 1 September 2000. Parents have to complete a *notice of appeal* and send it to SENT with any relevant supporting documentation. The notice of appeal is followed by simultaneous presentations of *statements of case* with written evidence from parents and the LEA within 30 working days of the notice of appeal being sent to SENT. Hearings take place in private. Late evidence will be accepted at the hearing, provided it is submitted in advance, and is not too lengthy. Children with SEN can submit evidence prior to the Tribunal hearing. They also have the right to attend SENT hearings and give evidence on their own behalf. A decision is usually given orally at the end of the hearing, or reserved for up to ten days. A written decision is recorded and signed. Either party can appeal against the SENT decision within ten working days. Class teachers or subject teachers may contribute evidence for a statement of case about the progress, or lack of progress, a SEN pupil has made in relation to their IEP targets.

SENT will accept appeals:	SENT will not deal with cases concerning:
when the LEA refuses: – to make a statutory assessment – to issue a statement – to change the school named on the statement. Parents can also appeal against: – the description of the child's SEN on the statement – the planned SEN provision for the child described on the statement – an existing statement not naming the school – the LEA ceasing to maintain a statement.	– the way the school is meeting the child's SEN – whether the school is following the SEN Code of Practice and meeting the child's needs – the length of time it has taken the LEA to assess or statement the child – the way in which the assessment was done – the way in which the LEA arranges for the child to be helped.

What are the National SEN Specialist Standards? The TTA introduced the National SEN Specialist Standards in December 1999. The Standards are set out in four sections. NQTs will find the Core Standards and the skills and attributes most relevant to them.

National SEN Specialist Standards

Core Standards

These are relevant to all teachers working with SEN pupils in a range of educational settings. They cover:
- strategic direction and development of SEN provision nationally and regionally, e.g. SEN legislation, inclusion, equal opportunities, disability rights, operation of local SEN agencies;
- identification, assessment and planning, e.g. how assessment informs curriculum planning, use of IEPs to judge pupil progress, preparing and writing accurate assessment reports;
- effective teaching and ensuring maximum curriculum access, e.g. reduce barriers to learning, differentiate the curriculum;
- development of communication, literacy and numeracy skills and ICT capability;
- promotion of social and emotional development, positive behaviour and preparation for adulthood, e.g. use of reward systems, pupil mentoring, alternative accreditation.

Skills and attributes required by all teachers working with pupils with severe and/or complex SEN in a range of school settings

- High expectations of pupils with severe and/or complex forms of SEN.
- Acceptance that all pupils are entitled to a broad, balanced, relevant and differentiated curriculum.
- Willingness to collaborate with other professionals.
- Willingness to adapt teaching strategies.
- Readiness to work alongside other teachers, and with parents/carers.
- Sensitivity to, and professionalism in discussing and reporting individual learning and developmental difficulties.
- Appreciation of the contribution different professional groups make to the provision for SEN pupils with more severe and/or complex needs.

Inclusive Schools and Newly Appointed Teachers

Schools are required to have a clear policy for the induction of newly appointed staff. Within the Index for Inclusion (Centre for Studies in Inclusive Education (CSIE) 2000), CSIE outlines how schools can help new staff settle in, by answering a series of questions.

Dimension B: Producing inclusive policies
Section 1 – Developing a school for all
Indicator: B.1.2 All new staff are helped to settle in to the school.

- Does the school recognise the difficulties that new staff may have in settling into a new job in what may be a new locality?
- Do longer serving staff avoid making new staff feel outsiders, for example by the use of a 'we' or an 'us' which excludes them?
- Does every new member of staff have a mentor who is genuinely interested in helping him or her to settle into the school?
- Does the school make new staff feel that the experience and knowledge they bring to the school is valued?
- Are there opportunities for all staff to share their knowledge and expertise so that this includes contributions from new staff?
- Are new staff provided with the basic information they need about the school?
- Are new staff asked about what additional information they need, and is it provided?
- Are the observations about the school of new staff sought and valued for the fresh insights that they contain?

(CSIE 2000: 24)

Part 2

Core Concerns and Selected Strategies

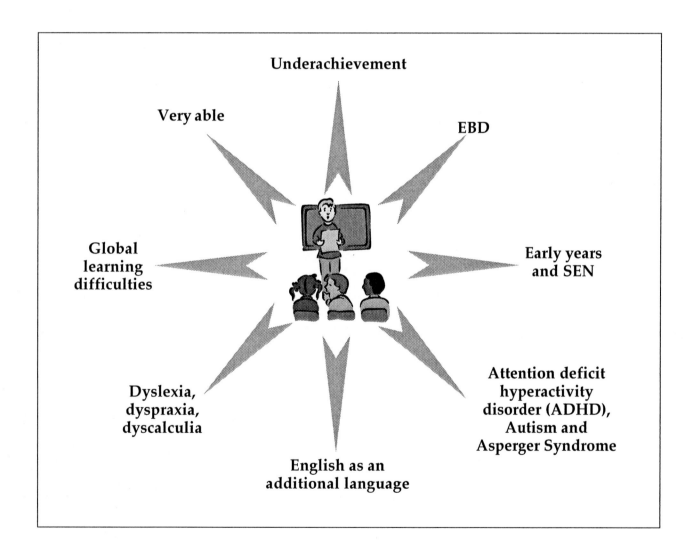

Underachievement

What is underachievement?

Underachievement arises when there is a mismatch between actual achievement and expected achievement.

Who are the underachievers?

- Those with specific learning difficulties.
- Those whose first language is not English.
- Boys, or girls, influenced by stereotypical or cultural factors.
- More able pupils hiding their high ability from other peers.

What are the signs of underachievement?

- Inconsistent pattern of achievement.
- Discrepancy between ability and achievement – poor test performance.
- Daydreaming.
- Avoiding success in work.
- Talking in class, 'clowning', to delay starting work.
- Boredom.
- Withdrawal.
- Poor concentration.
- Reluctance to do written work.
- Work incomplete and poorly presented.

How to prevent underachievement

- Deliver well organised and highly structured lessons.
- Vary the pace of the lesson.
- Offer a range of stimulating, exciting and interesting activities.
- Make explanations and instructions clear.
- Support pupils' writing, e.g. use writing frames, brainstorming, flow charts.
- Provide short, focused tasks.
- Motivate by using ICT.
- Provide a learning mentor or a peer 'study buddy'.
- Include group working opportunities.
- Give immediate praise and reward for effort and progress.

> Difficult behaviour sometimes results from unidentified or unmet special educational needs, including Emotional and Behavioural Difficulties. Identifying the need and taking preventative action, including involving the Special Educational Needs Co-ordinator, may prevent problems escalating and produce changes for the better.   (DfEE 1999d: para. 3.1)

Emotional and Behavioural Difficulties

The Circular on social inclusion goes on to add:

> Effective early intervention can also prevent emerging problems from becoming special educational needs. As soon as there are difficulties, staff should liaise with the SENCO so that known SEN can be taken into account or consideration be given to whether the child has unidentified or unmet SEN – such as dyslexia or problems of attention and hyperactivity – and needs to be placed on the SEN Register.
> (DfEE 1999d: para. 3.2)

EBD Criteria

QCA and DfEE have developed assessment criteria for pupils aged 5–16 with emotional and behavioural difficulties. They were published in January 2001, with accompanying guidance. The assessment criteria demonstrate the progress of pupils' emotional and behavioural development as positive outcomes. The desirable behaviour domains that the assessment criteria cover relate to: conduct behaviour, learning behaviour and emotional behaviour. The QCA/DfEE criteria are useful for target setting on EBD IEPs and Pastoral Support Programmes.

Index for Inclusion and EBD pupils

In the Index for Inclusion (CSIE 2000), CSIE focuses on improving classroom behaviour in order to remove barriers to learning. (Dimension C: Evolving inclusive practices – Indicator C.1.7 *'Classroom discipline is based on mutual respect'*, is outlined on the next page.)

C.1 Orchestrating Learning

Indicator C.1.7: Classroom discipline is based on mutual respect

   (i)   Does the approach to discipline encourage self-discipline?

   (ii) Do staff support each other to be assertive without being angry?

   (iii) Do staff share their concerns and pool their knowledge and skills in overcoming disaffection and disruption?

   (iv) Are classroom routines consistent and explicit?

   (v)   Are students involved in helping to resolve classroom difficulties?

   (vi) Are students involved in formulating classroom rules?

   (vii) Are students consulted on how to improve the classroom atmosphere?

   (viii) Are students consulted on how to improve attention to learning?

   (ix) If there is more than one adult in the room do they share responsibilities for the smooth running of lessons?

   (x)   Are there clear procedures, understood by students and teachers for responding to extremes of challenging behaviour?

   (xi) Is it recognised by all staff and students that it is unfair for boys to take up more of a teacher's attention than girls?

(CSIE 2000: 83)

Meeting the Needs of Pupils with Behavioural Difficulties

Managing pupil behaviour is a major aspect of teaching that causes anxieties to ITT students and NQTs. EBD are a continuum of behaviours from that which is unacceptable and challenges teachers, but is within the norm, to that which indicates serious mental illness.

Children with EBD have special educational needs and learning difficulties as a result of their behaviour causing a barrier to learning and impeding curriculum access. EBD pupils may be withdrawn, depressed, frustrated, aggressive, anti-social, or manifest self-injurious tendencies.

Why pupils misbehave

- **Family factors** – abuse, neglect, divorce/separation, illness/death, deprivation.
- **Child-centred factors** – lack of confidence, low self-esteem, poor social skills, tiredness, sensory/physical impairment, specific learning difficulties.
- **School factors** – inappropriate curriculum, insufficient rewards, lessons too long, inconsistent behaviour management by teachers.
- **Classroom factors** – little curriculum differentiation, inappropriate work set, unclear instructions/explanations, poorly planned lessons, little variety in teaching style, little pupil participation, poor pupil grouping.

> We point out the links between the content and methods of delivery of the school's curriculum, and the motivation and behaviour of pupils, . . . they require stimulating and suitably differentiated programmes of study.
>
> (Elton Report (DES 1989): para.13)

Key characteristics

Minor behaviour problems	Serious behaviour problems
• Calling out	• Swearing
• Being off task	• Destroying the work of peers
• Being out of seat	• Making sexual/racial comments
• Throwing paper	• Vandalising books/equipment
• Distracting peers	• Violent, dangerous behaviour
• Arriving late to lesson	• Lacking respect for others
• Answering back, cheeky	• Bullying
• Talking when the teacher talks	• Fighting
• Not listening to the teacher	• Persistent lying
• Forgetting equipment	• Walking out of the class

> Set high expectations for pupils' behaviour, establishing and maintaining a good standard of discipline through well focused teaching and through positive and productive relationships.   (QTS Standards; DfEE 1998a: Annex A, 4:i)

ABC of behaviour

To find out why pupils keep manifesting particular behaviour, it is useful to undertake an *ABC analysis*.

Antecedents:	Events happening before the behaviour appears.
Behaviour:	The actual behaviour.
Consequences:	What happens afterwards. How does the pupil feel? How do others react?

Practical solutions

- Listen to pupils. Give them time to explain their misbehaviour.
- Handle misbehaviour quickly and calmly to minimise disruption. Don't over-react.
- Move round the classroom, constantly scanning the class for misbehaviour.
- Avoid confrontation. Change the subject, defuse the situation, use humour and negotiate.
- Display classroom rules. Phrase the rules positively, refer to them regularly and be consistent.
- Condemn and criticise the misbehaviour and *not* the child.
- Catch the pupil being good. Emphasise the positive.
- Reprimand pupils privately. Don't humiliate them publicly.
- Reward good behaviour instantly with praise and encouragement, and award stars, ticks, and stickers.
- Gain pupils' attention by stopping talking mid-sentence. Say something unexpected: say the pupil's name, make a joke or say 'Look at me', 'Listen' or 'Excuse me'.
- Use non-verbal cues: raising eyebrows, frowning, being silent, making direct eye contact, moving near the pupil, using silence symbol cards, putting finger to lips or moving the pupil to the front of the class.
- Give the pupil a classroom responsibility.
- Ensure that lessons are well structured and appropriately differentiated, and that clear and concise instructions and explanations are given.
- Provide an opportunity for 'time out' or 'cooling off', e.g. use of computer.

> Secures a good standard of pupil behaviour in the classroom through establishing appropriate rules and high expectations of discipline which pupils respect, acting to pre-empt and deal with inappropriate behaviour in the context of the behaviour policy of the school.
>
> (NQT Induction Standards; DfEE 1999a: Annex A, 2:c)

Attention Deficit Hyperactivity Disorder (ADHD)

This is an inherited condition, more common in boys, which results in inattention, impulsiveness, hyperactivity and daydreaming. These children cannot help misbehaving. Some may be prescribed 'Ritalin' to modify their behaviour.

Children with more Complex and Challenging Behaviour

Key characteristics

Children with ADHD:
- have a short attention span, poor concentration and difficulty following instructions
- are easily distracted and have difficulty listening
- are forgetful, disorganised and lose books and homework
- take time to settle down to work
- act without thinking and are impatient
- take risks and are excitable
- are restless and fidgety, and wander around the classroom
- are argumentative and interrupt
- are attention seeking
- experience mood swings and are immature
- are erratic, and show spasmodic academic progress.

Practical solutions

- Raise the pupil's self-esteem by setting achievable tasks, and giving regular feedback about progress.
- Provide the pupil with a diary or tick list to remind them of what tasks need to be completed by when.
- Keep instructions, routines and rules short, concise, clear and positive.
- Ask the pupil to repeat what you have asked them to do to check understanding.
- Sit the pupil near the front of the class away from the distractions of doors and windows.
- Present work in small, manageable steps and give breaks in between tasks.
- Give the pupil interesting, stimulating curriculum materials to sustain interest.
- Quickly remove a pupil experiencing a temper tantrum from the rest of the class. Talk calmly to them. Get them back on task as soon as possible.
- Do not let the pupil know they have upset you or made you angry. Appear cool and calm.
- Ensure pupils have recorded homework correctly.

Autism

Approximately 26,000 children are autistic. Autism (a physical dysfunction of the brain) disrupts the development of social and communication skills. The autistic child has difficulty with social relationships, difficulty communicating and difficulty in the development of play, imagination and social understanding. Autistic children often have accompanying learning difficulties.

Key characteristics

Autistic children:
- have difficulty understanding and using language
- have obsessions, and think and talk about one topic of interest
- interpret speech literally, e.g. if told 'Pull your socks up', the child will
- don't make eye contact
- prefer to be socially isolated from other peers
- don't like any change in routine and cannot cope with this
- are aloof, indifferent to others and withdrawn
- manifest bizarre, eccentric behaviour and may make strange noises
- have poor comprehension skills.

Practical solutions

- Ensure that you obtain the pupil's full attention in the lesson.
- Break down tasks into smaller steps and stages.
- Give the pupil time to think before they answer a question.
- Maintain pupil attention by using expressions like 'keep looking'.
- Never comment on their failure to do a task. Show the pupil how to do the task.
- Explain instructions clearly and repeat them.
- Provide relatively easy tasks to ensure successful completion at first.
- Start the next activity straight away after the pupil has been successful.
- Position the pupil in an area of the classroom with few distractions.
- Use a variety of teaching approaches and activities throughout the lesson to maintain interest.
- If the pupil becomes restless or agitated, offer an alternative activity, e.g. use of the computer.

Asperger Syndrome

Children with Asperger Syndrome have higher academic and linguistic ability than autistic children. It is more common among boys than girls.

Asperger Syndrome is a genetic brain dysfunction resulting in a disorder of personality. 75% of children with Asperger Syndrome also have a specific learning difficulty.

Key characteristics

Children with Asperger Syndrome:
- are socially isolated from peers by personal choice
- can behave in a socially inappropriate way
- use formal, pedantic speech with an expressionless voice
- stick to routines
- experience difficulty transferring skills from one situation to another
- may be clumsy
- have poor organisational skills
- have difficulty with written recording
- often do not finish tasks
- exhibit obsessive compulsive behaviour
- have difficulty making friends.

Practical solutions

- Break down tasks into smaller steps.
- Sequence activities.
- Identify the main idea in new information.
- Use prompts to enable the pupil to commence tasks.
- Check that the pupil understands what they have to do.
- Give one instruction at a time.
- Introduce choice in tasks gradually to develop decision-making skills.
- Show the pupil what is expected by demonstration.
- Use visual or pictorial cues to make a task clear and aid understanding.
- Be calm, positive and consistent with the pupil.
- Identify the pupil's interests and likes and incorporate these into curriculum activities.
- Introduce any change gradually to the pupil.

Specific Learning Difficulties

What are specific learning difficulties?

> A specific learning difficulty is neurologically based and causes problems with managing verbal codes in memory. This hinders the learning of literacy skills, and can affect other symbolic systems such as musical notation and mathematics.
>
> (Dyslexia Institute 1999)

Specific learning difficulties (SpLD) include dyslexia, dyscalculia and dyspraxia. One key indicator of SpLD is the disparity between a child's chronological age and their reading age; i.e. a reading age of two years or more below their chronological age, and in relation to their average, or above average ability.

In a recent report on SpLD, OFSTED made the following recommendations, which NQTs and ITT students would be wise to note:

> Pupils with specific learning difficulties should not be expected to complete the same reading and writing tasks as other pupils of similar ability in the class, but should be provided with modified assignments which make allowances for their particular learning difficulties.   (OFSTED 1999b: para. 30)

OFSTED further suggests:

> Alternative provision for pupils with specific learning difficulties might include group reading and discussion of the text, the use of video material, the presentation of work in forms other than writing, and the use of suitable notes summarising the work covered, which might also serve to aid revision for examinations.   (OFSTED 1999b: para. 31)

David Blunkett commented:

> The effects of dyslexia can be alleviated by using appropriate teaching strategies and committed learning.
>
> (DfEE/BDA 1999c: Foreword)

Dyslexia

> If dyslexia was better catered for within all mainstream schools we could avoid the massive problems of behavioural difficulty, poor self-esteem and underachievement.   (McKeown 1999: 19)

What is dyslexia?

Dyslexia is difficulty with words and acquiring literacy skills. Dyslexia can be inherited or acquired through illness or accident. More boys than girls have dyslexia. Dyslexics have both sides of the brain equally developed, instead of the left side of brain being more developed, which deals with processing speech and language. Dyslexia affects children of all abilities.

Features of dyslexia

Children with dyslexia:
- reverse letters and words
- use bizarre spellings
- have poor reading skills: slow rate or omitting or misreading words
- have poor letter/word recognition
- have poor memory
- have difficulty copying from the board
- have left and right confusion
- have poor organisational skills
- have difficulty sequencing ideas on paper, or committing ideas to paper
- have poor concentration and difficulty listening
- experience fatigue and frustration in learning
- have untidy written work and poor handwriting
- have oral skills better than their written language
- have difficulty with musical notation.

Improving curriculum access for dyslexic pupils

- Break down tasks, information, instructions into smaller parts.
- Ensure that differentiated work matches reading level and is age appropriate.
- Display key words/subject vocabulary on classroom walls, and provide word banks.
- Provide photocopied notes, and highlight or underline key words and phrases in the text.
- Allow alternative methods of recording, e.g. computer, verbal response, graphical representation, scribe.
- Give extra time for completing written tasks at home and in class.
- Provide support for writing, e.g. writing frames, grids, flow diagrams, brainstorming, model/demonstrate.
- Write homework down for pupils and repeat instructions.
- Make use of rhymes, acronyms or visual methods to aid memory.
- Mark work on content rather than on spelling.

Dyscalculia

What is dyscalculia?

Dyscalculia is a difficulty with numbers arising from a deficiency in the mathematical ability of the brain. Some pupils with dyscalculia may also be dyslexic.

Features of dyscalculia

Children with dyscalculia:
- make errors in carrying numbers over
- ignore decimal points
- experience confusion recognising and using mathematical signs/symbols
- confuse left and right when undertaking calculations like division
- need concrete mathematics apparatus
- have difficulty learning and remembering multiplication tables
- experience difficulties with problem-solving tasks in mathematics
- set out calculations untidily and incorrectly
- have difficulty telling the time by an analogue clock or watch
- have difficulty working out the correct change from a given sum of money
- have a tendency to reverse and transpose numbers
- experience problems in sequencing numbers
- have difficulty recognising/naming shapes and patterns.

Strategies to improve mathematical skills

- Put a list of numbers with their spellings (1–100) on a prompt card.
- Give the pupil a set of mathematics symbol cards with the range of names for each symbol.
- Provide an audio tape with multiplication tables on for home/class use.
- Provide support materials, e.g. number square, number line, calculator, counters, large decimal point.
- Head number columns (Hundreds, Tens, Units) to assist with place value.
- Use arrows to help pupils know which direction to perform a calculation in.
- Model a method of calculation and put this in the pupil's exercise book.
- Allow the pupil to use their own method of calculation if it produces the correct answer consistently.
- Break down mathematics problems into smaller steps.
- If the pupil is also dyslexic, audio tape 'wordy' problem solving questions.

Dyspraxia

What is dyspraxia?

Children who are dyspraxic are clumsy, uncoordinated, and experience organisational difficulties. More boys than girls are dyspraxic.

Features of dyspraxia

Children with dyspraxia:
- have writing that is slow, poorly sized, untidy, off-the-line
- have poor hand–eye coordination
- have difficulty using scissors, cutting-out, tracing shapes, drawing a straight line
- have poor balance and posture
- have poor listening skills
- have poor memory retention
- have short concentration span
- have difficulty putting puzzles together
- have poor concept of shapes
- have weak sequencing skills
- confuse left and right
- have difficulty following instructions and understanding positional language
- have immature, silly behaviour as a result of frustration in learning.

Strategies to support dyspraxic pupils' learning

- Break down tasks and instructions into smaller parts.
- Pair a dyspraxic pupil with a more coordinated supportive peer in practical activities.
- Use pictures, symbols, modelling and demonstration.
- Repeat instructions.
- Write homework down for the pupil.
- Praise effort and attainment, however small.
- Provide additional time during practical tasks.
- Cut out shapes for pupils beforehand.
- Encourage the pupil to self-correct their own work or behaviour.
- Use colour coding for left and right.

Very Able Pupils

Who are the very able?

> The very able are defined as those who either demonstrate exceptionally high-level performance, whether across a range of endeavours or in a limited field, or those whose potential for excellence has not yet been recognised by either tests or experts.   (OFSTED 1998b: 1)

Very able pupils are likely to be working within the upper levels of a key stage, or be one key stage ahead.

Very able pupils may display other aptitudes such as: artistic, creative or physical talents; mechanical ingenuity; visual and performing abilities; outstanding leadership and social awareness.

How many pupils are very able?

The number of pupils identified is dependent on the ethos and culture of the school. An inclusive school, which recognises and celebrates a diversity of pupil ability is likely to encourage more pupils to reach their full potential. As a guide, in an average school pupil population:

- 2 per cent at least are likely to be exceptional and outstanding all-rounders (intelligence quotient (IQ) 130+)
- 18 per cent are likely to be gifted and talented in one or two subjects (IQ 115–129).

The DfEE 'Excellence in Cities' initiative (DfEE 1999e) targets the highest performing 5–10 per cent of pupils in secondary schools.

IQ as a means of identification should be viewed with caution, as it does not show pupils' creativity. Therefore, a range of identification strategies should be employed, which are inclusive and not exclusive.

How are the very able identified? Identification strategies

- General and subject specific checklists.
- Biographical details from parents.
- Nomination by teachers, parents, other pupils, self- or peer nomination.
- Standardised test information: e.g. cognitive ability tests (CATs), standard assessment tasks (SATs), General Certificate of Secondary Education (GCSE), non-verbal reasoning tests.
- Teacher assessment: subject reports, records of achievement (RoAs), samples of work.
- Provision: pupils able to excel when given challenging learning opportunities.

Characteristics of very able pupils

Very able pupils:
- are inquisitive and ask searching questions
- learn quickly
- are imaginative
- have good memories
- have extensive general knowledge
- are mature for their age
- are self-confident
- are perfectionists
- are intuitive
- are quick thinkers
- are precocious
- become absorbed and engrossed in learning.

How are the very able perceived?

Pupil perceptions

I get fed up waiting for the others in the class to catch up.

A lot of the class work I do is boring, and I want to be able to think for myself.

Teacher perceptions

The most able pupil in my class always finishes their work first. I never know what to give them to do next.

I worry that the most able pupil in the class will ask me a question I don't know the answer to. I feel I am expected to know everything as the teacher.

Changing the culture

A loner – absorbed in their learning.

Passionate and knowledgeable about their subject.

Studious

Spends hours in the library.

Schools and classrooms need to promote an inclusive culture

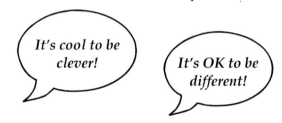

It's cool to be clever!

It's OK to be different!

How can the needs of the very able be met?

Very able pupils like SEN pupils can benefit from individual tuition and mentoring, in-class support, self-supported study using ICT and the Internet, and have IEPs with challenging targets.

Three ways to help the very able reach their optimum potential are:

Enrichment	Extension	Acceleration
Broader and more varied curriculum learning experiences that enable the pupil to be aware of the wider context of the subject, and use higher level thinking skills.	Deepening of the curriculum to stretch and challenge the pupil.	Pupil progressing at a faster rate through the school, i.e. moving up a year or phase earlier. It can also refer to the pace of instruction.

HMI recommended that curriculum differentiation for the very able be done:
- by outcome, giving a common task to elicit different levels of response
- by rate of progress, allowing a pupil to proceed through a course at his or her own speed
- by enrichment, giving a pupil supplementary tasks intended to broaden or deepen skills and understanding
- by setting different tasks requiring greater sophistication within a common theme or topic.

(HMI 1992: para. 37)

How do I meet the needs of the very able?

Some suggested classroom strategies

- Set a quiz question, a problem of the week, or an unusual word to define.
- Run class competitions, e.g. creative writing, design a classroom poster, invent a useful classroom gadget.
- Set more challenging, inventive tasks, e.g. devise their own crossword or word search, or devise their own questions to a given list of answers.
- Have a 'question of the week' envelope or box, to encourage more reticent able pupils to ask more challenging questions.
- Use plenty of open questions and set open-ended tasks, e.g. 'Imagine you are a . . .', 'What would happen if . . .', 'Can you think of another way to . . .'
- Give them real-life problem solving activities to enable them to hypothesise, explore different solutions and modify solutions.
- Provide opportunities that develop thinking skills: observation, exploration, comparison, classification, imagination, prediction, critical thinking, interpretation, summarising, reflection and evaluation.
- Provide a range of tasks that develop their analytical skills, e.g. investigative report writing, research activities through detective work, at the scene of the crime – reporting back.
- Give them the chance to plan, select, analyse and discuss their own work.
- Put challenges on their learning, e.g. set time limits for task completion, or word limits.
- Use a wider range of curriculum materials from later key stages or higher levels of study.
- Use more difficult challenging texts to extend their subject specific vocabulary and develop their study skills.
- Encourage them to use more sophisticated and complex vocabulary.
- Provide opportunities for collaborative group work, role play, hot-seating activities.
- Give them a choice in how they present their findings, e.g. diary account, newspaper report, interview, graphical presentations.
- Make use of positive role models – inviting external subject experts in to work with the class.
- Set homework which is more demanding and challenging and develops their research skills.
- Provide opportunities for visits to museums, exhibition centres, art galleries, or attendance at master classes, Saturday classes.
- Seek opportunities to foster cross-phase learning links.

Global Learning Difficulties

What are global learning difficulties?

Global learning difficulties refer to pupils who experience a general learning delay in all areas of development, which is significant enough to cause the child problems in keeping up with the rest of the class.

Key characteristics

Children with global learning difficulties:
- have a poor concentration span
- are over-dependent on the teacher and LSA
- seek constant reassurance when doing their work
- have a poor self-image, poor self-esteem and lack self-confidence
- have poor listening skills
- have difficulty remembering lengthy or complex instructions
- have poor organisational skills
- are slow in completing tasks
- are reluctant to read aloud or perform in front of other peers
- have poor comprehension and basic skill level
- have written work that is poorly presented and untidy.

Some practical solutions

- Use a structured, step-by-step teaching approach.
- Break down tasks into smaller stages, giving one stage at a time.
- Simplify instructions and write them down for the pupil.
- Provide short breaks and 'time out' between activities.
- Check their learning by asking them to explain back to you what they have done, or relate what they have learnt.
- Provide plenty of opportunities for over-learning.
- Ensure that activities are interesting and within their capabilities.
- Pair up the pupil with a more able supportive peer.
- Use real-life objects or examples.
- Reward and praise pupil for their effort/achievement; celebrate success.
- Set closed tasks and questions for homework.

What is EAL?

EAL acknowledges that pupils may have knowledge of more than one other home or community language. EAL is mainly about teaching and learning English language through the content of the whole curriculum. About 200 different languages are used throughout England.

Bilingual pupils' first language development supports the learning of the second or additional language (English). It can take a bilingual pupil up to seven years to acquire the proficiency in academic English required for GCSE.

Who are EAL pupils?

They are children:
- born outside the UK in non-English speaking communities
- born in the UK but not exposed to the English language at home.

What is it like being an EAL pupil?

It is a similar experience to being abroad on holiday and not being able to communicate in the foreign language of that country.

EAL pupils have to 'catch up' with their English speaking peers in relation to learning:
- a new language
- the curriculum in English
- the values and customs associated with English, alongside their own home culture and background.

> **HEALTH CHECK**
>
> Don't assume that because a pupil does not speak English fluently that they have a learning difficulty.

EAL pupils have the same academic potential, irrespective of their first language.

EAL and SEN

An EAL pupil may experience special educational needs if they:
- can't keep up with peers who speak the same 'mother tongue'
- experience difficulties in subjects like Art, PE and Music
- are not speaking any English after being exposed to the language for six months or more
- make minimal progress, despite having the additional support of a bilingual assistant.

English as an Additional Language (EAL)

29

Class and subject teachers' roles and responsibilities for EAL

- Be knowledgeable about pupils' abilities and their needs in English and other subjects.
- Use this knowledge effectively in curriculum planning, classroom teaching and pupil grouping.
- Make good use of specialist language support teachers and bilingual assistants when teaching and monitoring progress.

(QCA 2000a: 6)

Improving curriculum access for EAL pupils

- Give them the opportunity to use their first language in learning, and to then transfer their knowledge to English.
- Use plenty of visual clues and real objects: video, pictures, charts, maps, information and communications technology (ICT).
- Have dual textbooks and reading books available.
- Ensure that the classroom displays show cultural diversity and dual labelling.
- Use dual word banks and bilingual dictionaries.
- Provide collaborative activities that involve talking and role play.
- Place EAL pupils in supportive groups with expert peer readers and writers who can 'model' the required skills.
- Give them the opportunity to report back to others.
- Provide opportunities for over-learning, e.g. use repetitive language activities like sentence matching and sequencing, and games in order to revisit skills and key concepts.
- Support writing activities by using brainstorming and writing frames.
- Allow EAL pupils to draft a piece of writing in their first language, to support their English.
- Model key language features and structures by demonstration.

Teachers assessing pupils learning EAL should:
- recognise what pupls can do and reward achievement
- ensure it is a valid reflection of what has been taught or covered in class
- be clear about the purpose of the assessment – summative, formative or diagnostic
- be sensitive to the pupil's first or main other language(s) and heritage culture
- take account of how long the pupil has been learning English
- assess in ways that are appropriate to the pupils' ages
- focus on language, while being aware of the influence of behaviour, attitude and cultural expectations
- recognise that pupils may be at different levels of attainment in speaking, listening, reading and writing.

(QCA 2000a: 7–8)

September 2000 saw the introduction of the QCA early learning goals (QCA 1999) for children at the foundation stage (from 3 years to 6 years – end of Reception). The purpose of the goals is to provide a more structured curriculum framework with specific targets.

The six main areas to the foundation stage curriculum are:

Early Years and SEN

- personal, social and emotional development
- communication, language and literacy
- mathematical development
- knowledge and understanding of the world
- physical development
- creative development.

Baseline assessment, first introduced in September 1998, to assess children as they begin their primary education, can highlight where a child may have learning difficulties, which require further attention and targeted teaching.

> Some children's special needs – for example, moderate or specific learning difficulties (including dyslexia) – may not emerge until children start school . . . Baseline assessment will not, on its own, establish whether individual pupils have SEN. But the information from such assessments will help teachers plan to meet the learning needs of every pupil, including those with SEN. (DfEE 1998b: 1.5)

Early identification of SEN in the foundation stage, along with the appropriate intervention, is crucial in enabling those children to succeed in later life. Early years teachers have a key role to play in identifying individual learning needs, and removing any barriers to learning.

According to QCA, children with SEN can make the best possible progress if early years staff:

- Use signs, symbols, visual materials, audio tapes, ICT to facilitate communication;
- Use multi-sensory teaching approaches and word descriptions to develop understanding;
- Use a range of teaching strategies to match children's individual learning needs;
- Use a range of learning materials which reflect diversity;
- Provide additional adult support, modify and adapt activities, use specialist aids and equipment to increase participation in physical and practical activity;
- Establish clear boundaries for behaviour, praise efforts, assist children to respect and value the contributions of others;
- Build upon children's previous knowledge, experiences, interests and competencies;
- Plan challenging opportunities for more able children;
- Provide a safe and supportive learning environment.

(QCA 1999: 13–14)

Part 3

Planning Progress

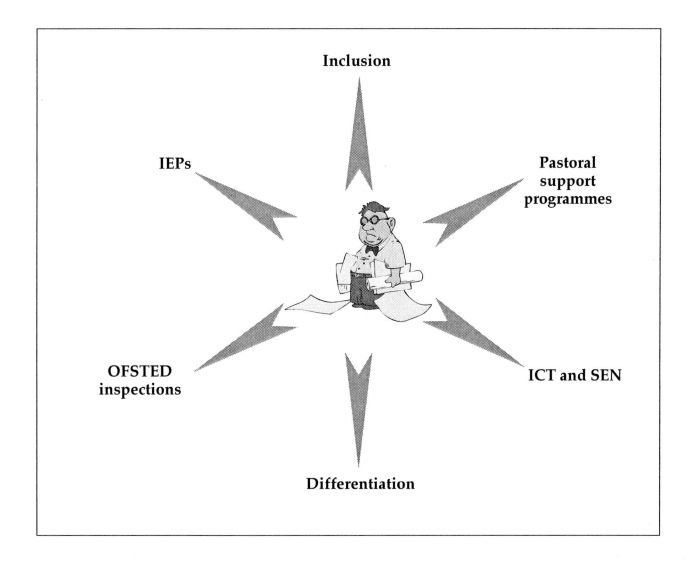

Meeting a Diversity of Needs in the Inclusive Classroom

> Pupils with SEN should have the same opportunities as others to progress and demonstrate achievement.   (DfEE 1997b: 1:24)

Teachers and ITT students must challenge low expectations and differentiate the curriculum to meet a diversity of needs.

The SEN Code of Practice (1994) saw increased differentiation taking place within the pupil's normal classroom work.

> All newly qualified teachers will be able to differentiate teaching practice appropriately.   (DfEE 1997b: 6:5)

> **Differentiation matches what is taught and how it is taught to individual pupil's needs and learning styles.**

Differentiation is synonymous with inclusion and good teaching. It builds on pupils' past achievement and provides challenge for further achievement and opportunities for successful learning.

Differentiation is about intervening to maximise pupil potential, and to ensure curriculum access and entitlement.

> **Inclusion is a process that develops ways of increasing the participation and learning of all pupils and minimises barriers to their learning and participation.**

The new school inspection framework introduced in January 2000 places greater emphasis on educational inclusion. It focuses on the impact of teaching on pupils' learning, how well pupils make progress, and the extent to which teachers use methods that enable pupils of all abilities to learn effectively.

> Plans effectively to ensure that pupils have the opportunity to meet their potential, not withstanding differences of race and gender, taking account of the needs of pupils who are underachieving, very able, not yet fluent in English.
>   (NQT Induction Standards; DfEE 1999a: Annex A: 2b)

For all key stages, Curriculum 2000 stipulates three essential principles to developing a more inclusive curriculum:

1. **Setting suitable learning challenges**
   - Select curriculum from earlier or later key stages to suit the pupil's abilities.
   - Use increased differentiation with low attainers.
   - Extend the breadth and depth of study by further differentiation for high attainers.

2. **Responding to pupils' diverse learning needs**
   - Plan teaching and learning to match pupils' different learning experiences and strengths.
   - Value the contributions of all pupils.
   - Secure pupils' motivation and concentration.
   - Use teaching approaches appropriate to different learning styles.
   - Use a range of organisational approaches (i.e. setting, grouping, individual work).
   - Vary subject content and presentation to match learning needs.
   - Plan work that builds on pupils' interests and cultural experiences.
   - Plan challenging work for pupils whose ability and understanding is in advance of their language skills.
   - Plan and monitor the pace of work.

3. **Overcoming potential barriers to learning**
   - Use texts that pupils can read and understand.
   - Use visual materials, e.g. signs/symbols, video, photographs, pictograms.
   - Use ICT and audio taped materials.
   - Use adult/peer scribes.
   - Use role play.
   - Allow pupils time to learn, and gradually increase the range of activities and the learning demands once the pupil experiences success.

Barriers to learning

- Poor curriculum delivery.
- Little if any appropriate differentiation.
- Curriculum not relevant to pupil's experiences.
- Poorly prepared lessons.
- Use of unfamiliar language, technical vocabulary.
- Negative teacher attitudes towards pupils with diverse and complex needs.
- Little teacher explanation of key concepts, instructions and tasks provided.
- Lack of opportunity for pupil participation.
- Didactic, boring, uninspiring teaching.
- Disruption to lessons from poorly behaved pupils.

> Use teaching methods which sustain the momentum of pupils' work and keep all pupils engaged through matching the approaches used to the subject matter and the pupils being taught. (QTS Standards; DfEE 1999a: Annex A: 4k.ii)

Index for inclusion

March 2000 saw the launch of the Index for Inclusion (CSIE 2000), originally designed exclusively for use with SEN pupils in mainstream schools. It covers disabled children and ethnic minorities as well as SEN. Developed by the CSIE, Manchester University and Canterbury Christ Church University College, the key purpose of the Index for Inclusion is to encourage mainstream schools to value all pupils equally and celebrate diversity in an inclusive culture. The Index helps schools to identify inequality and barriers to learning, and tackle discrimination. It focuses on three dimensions of school life: A, Creating Inclusive Cultures; B, Producing Inclusive Policies; and C, Evolving Inclusive Practices. Each dimension is divided into two sections. Each section contains up to 12 indicators that are clarified by a series of questions.

Below is an example of the indicators within dimension C: Evolving Inclusive Practices.

Dimension C: Evolving inclusive PRACTICES
Section 1: C.1 Orchestrating learning

Indicators:

C.1.1   Lessons are responsive to student diversity.
C.1.2   Lessons are made accessible to all students.
C.1.3   Lessons develop an understanding of difference.
C.1.4   Students are actively involved in their own learning.
C.1.5   Students learn collaboratively.
C.1.6   Assessment encourages the achievements of all students.
C.1.7   Classroom discipline is based on mutual respect.
C.1.8   Teachers plan, review and teach in partnership.
C.1.9   Teachers are concerned to support the learning and participation of all students.
C.1.10 Learning support assistants are concerned to support the learning and participation of all students.
C.1.11 Homework contributes to the learning of all.
C.1.12 All students take part in activities outside the classroom.
(CSIE 2000: 48)

The indicators in dimension C.1. of the Index for Inclusion provide class/subject teachers with a valuable audit tool with which to reflect upon their teaching style and curriculum delivery.

> Pupils with specific learning difficulties need practical help and guidance to acquire appropriate study skills and to plan and organise their work effectively.   (OFSTED 1999b: para. 29)

Helping Pupils Develop Study Skills

Incorporating the teaching of study skills across the curriculum is important for ensuring pupils with a diversity of SEN reach their maximum potential.

Some practical strategies

- Teach visualisation strategies, e.g. pupils visualise their bedroom, with key words and/or facts placed on pieces of furniture in the room.
- Model how to take notes, showing pupils different strategies, e.g. margin notes, numbering key points, underlining, highlighting, and sketching main facts.
- Teach pupils how to skim and scan texts for information:
- *Skimming:* glancing through a text to get an overall idea of what it is about
- *Scanning:* quickly going through a text to find out specific information.
- Encourage pupils to use **DARTS** (Directed Activities Related to Text).

DARTS

Darts are a range of strategies to support learning and literacy across the curriculum. They enable pupils of all abilities to access texts more readily, extend their learning and deepen their understanding.

Darts are more effective when pupils work collaboratively.

The two main types of DARTS are:

- **Reconstruction activities:** pupils reconstruct a modified text by: cloze/gap-fill, prediction, text matching or sequencing.
- **Processing activities:** pupils transform and explore an original text themselves, using visual presentation of their information, presenting text in another form, and using grids to record key information.

Effective Differentiation

Teachers need to:

- know their class well, i.e. the diversity of pupil needs, individual needs, and the weaknesses, strengths and interests of pupils
- be aware of potential barriers to pupils learning
- have a secure knowledge of the subject
- work closely with other colleagues (LSAs, support teachers, SENCOs)
- know how to break down learning into smaller steps
- reflect on their own teaching practice and make necessary improvements
- know how children learn.

How children learn

Although children learn in different ways they are likely to learn more effectively when using their preferred learning style. Teachers therefore need to use a variety of teaching approaches that cover multi-sensory learning styles.

Three popular learning styles

The **visual learner**:

- likes drawing, writing and seeing images
- is very observant
- has a photographic memory
- likes the use of flow charts and spider diagrams

The **hearing learner**:

- is good at explaining things to others
- is an attentive listener
- has good recall of spoken information
- enjoys 'hot-seating', role play, debates, interviewing and oral comprehension

The **'touchy/feely' learner**:

- likes hands-on, practical activities, e.g. model making, experiments, investigative tasks
- learns best by doing and making things
- likes plenty of tactile learning experiences
- can become restless and 'switched off', fidget frequently and make little progress if tasks are not practical.

Ask some of your colleagues how they differentiate, and the most common response is 'by outcome'. However, there are several other methods of differentiation that you can use.

Methods of differentiation

- **Content/task**: a range of different activities/homework can be given on one subject.
- **Interest**: activities can relate to pupils' lifestyles/interests, i.e. music, food, fashion, sport.
- **Pace**: pupils can work at different rates on similar tasks.
- **Level**: pupils can use parallel graduated curriculum materials for the same subject area.
- **Access/resources**: pupils can carry out similar activities but use modified or additional materials and aids.
- **Response**: pupils can record outcomes in different ways, e.g. orally, writing, modelling, drawing.
- **Depth/sequence**: pupils can follow a common topic but study and develop different aspects of the topic further, e.g. World War II – food, fashion, leisure, family life.
- **Structure**: curriculum can be delivered to some pupils in smaller steps, while other pupils receive a section or unit all at once.
- **Support**: the teacher or LSA may give more individual time and attention to certain pupils, e.g. pupils with SEN, very able pupils and EAL pupils.
- **Teaching style**: the teacher can use a wider range of teaching approaches in a lesson.
- **Grouping**: pupils can work independently, in pairs, in small groups or as a whole-class group for particular activities.

Curriculum materials checklist

Worksheets and textbooks should:
- be relevant to pupils' interests and up-to-date
- be appropriate to the ability and reading level of the pupil
- be stimulating, interesting and visually appealing
- break up text with graphics, headings/sub-headings, charts
- be clear, in page layouts, with instructions and tasks in text using different font styles and sizes, and separated from each other on a page
- offer greater challenge and fun activities: games, puzzles, quizzes, word searches, crosswords
- use a range of activities: gap fill, matching, sequencing, labelling, true/false
- give opportunities for a range of responses, i.e. not just written answers.

Differentiated teaching approaches

All teachers, including ITT students on teaching practice, should reflect on their classroom teaching regularly, in order to evaluate if the methods employed are appropriate, and if a greater repertoire of teaching styles could be adopted, in order to meet a greater diversity of pupils' needs more effectively. NQTs and ITT students have the advantage of being observed by other more experienced teachers during their training and Induction year. This experience is valuable in obtaining practical advice about teaching methodology. In addition, observing other colleagues teaching can also provide further ideas for increasing your range of teaching approaches.

Below, is a list of some of the different teaching strategies you can use. It is always good practice to use a variety of teaching methods in any lesson, particularly when your class contains pupils with short attention spans, poor concentration levels, and little motivation to learn.

> What children with special needs so often require is not something radically different from other children ... but simply what all children need: a better and more vigorous curriculum pursued through a more varied and enlightened pedagogy.
>
> (Bell and Best 1986: 102)

Teaching methods

- Demonstration, modelling, example
- Audiovisual presentations
- Investigation and pupil research
- Visiting speakers
- Experiment and hypothesising
- Educational visits
- Case study
- Whole-class reading
- Practical tasks
- Board work
- Discussion/debate
- Use of library
- Questioning: open and closed
- Using real artefacts and concrete examples
- Explanation by teacher or pupils
- Problem-solving
- Comprehension tasks: oral and written
- Worksheets and handouts
- Role play and hot seating
- ICT
- Brainstorming
- Pupils planning and choosing activities
- Testing pupils
- Skill practice
- Revision: teacher instruction
- Team teaching
- Interviewing
- Independent work
- Pupil pair or group work
- Reporting back to the whole class
- Note-taking
- Textbook based tasks.

> ICT should be used to give children with special educational needs maximum access to the curriculum, and to help them reach their learning potential. (DfEE 1997b: 1:30)

ICT, SEN and Curriculum Access

> Trainees must be taught to recognise the specific contribution that ICT can make to teaching pupils with special educational needs in mainstream classrooms based upon the need to:
>
> a. provide access to the curriculum in a manner appropriate to pupils' needs;
> b. provide subject-specific support.
>
> (DfEE 1998a: Annex B: 5.)

National Curriculum 2000

The inclusion guidance for the National Curriculum 2000 emphasises the importance of pupils of all abilities applying and developing their ICT capability through the use of ICT tools and applications to support their learning across the curriculum.

OFSTED 2000

During school inspections, OFSTED inspectors will make judgements as to whether pupils are confident using ICT, and if activities are planned to develop pupils' ICT capability and support their learning, across the curriculum.

> Have a secure knowledge and understanding of ... ICT in subject teaching. (DfEE 1998a: Annex A: B1.b)
>
> Selecting and making good use of ... ICT ... to enable teaching objectives to be met. (DfEE 1998a: Annex A: B4k.ix)
>
> Exploiting opportunities to improve pupils basic skills in ICT. (QTS Standards, DfEE 1998a: Annex A: B4k.xi)

Advantages of ICT for SEN pupils

- The pupil is in control of their own learning.

- They are more confident in taking risks in learning.

- The computer is equitable and makes no judgements about the pupil's skills and knowledge.

ICT:

- motivates underachievers

- improves pupil concentration

- improves and develops basic literacy skills – writing, spelling, grammar, punctuation, drafting, proofreading, re-drafting – and extends vocabulary

- improves reading skills: enlarged font or text display and the voice-activated speech facility both help

- acts as a memory prompt and retains information and work on file

- improves communication, with email electronic conferencing for exchanging and sharing information

- raises self-esteem via the production of enhanced quality final pieces of work

- enhances study skills via skimming, scanning and summarising of text, information retrieval and research using the Internet

- improves hand–eye coordination for motor-impaired pupils, with joysticks, touch pads, track balls, head activated mouse

- provides multi-sensory learning opportunities for dyslexic pupils, who can look, listen and touch to improve letter and word recognition

- offers flexible learning opportunities across the curriculum via portable palm-top and laptop computers.

What is an IEP?

An IEP is an individual teacher action plan that details what, why and how often skills or items of knowledge should be taught to the pupil through 'additional' or 'extra' activities. It is regularly reviewed and evaluated so that identified targets can be reassessed, and informed judgements can be made about future learning and teaching.

Which pupils have an IEP?

SEN pupils at School Action, School Action Plus and those who are undergoing formal assessment, or who have a statement of SEN have an IEP. The class or subject teacher is responsible for contributing to the SEN pupil's IEP at the School Action stage and above.

Purpose of an IEP

The principal purpose of an IEP is to clarify what is to be done in the immediate short term to help the pupil make progress. IEPs increase learning opportunities for the SEN pupil by specifying which distinctive and different arrangements will be made for an individual pupil, as well as specifying the length and frequency of the additional provision.

The IEP will identify key skills to enhance the whole curriculum for SEN pupils. The IEP aims to move the pupil from what they can do to what is expected (provide challenge).

Key characteristics of an IEP

- It should focus on the specific learning/behavioural difficulties of the child;
- It should take account of what the child has already achieved, building on the curriculum the child is following;
- There should be clear targets to be achieved over a specific period of time;
- Both the child, and where possible the parent, should be involved in its preparation and review;
- The advice of outside specialists should be sought at Stage 3 (School Action Plus).   (OFSTED 1999c: para. 8)

The IEP should take account of the pupil's strengths and interests. IEPs contribute to the assessment of pupils and to their educational progress.

> IEPs are generally most helpful when they are crisply written, focusing on three or four short-term targets for the child, typically targets relating to key skills, such as communication skills, literacy, numeracy, behaviour and social skills, with dates for review.   (DfEE 1998b: 2.6)

Individual Education Plans and Target Setting

Features of a good IEP

Good IEPs will:
- Be seen as working documents;
- Use a simple format;
- Specify only provision and targets which are extra and additional to those generally available for, or expected to be achieved by, all pupils;
- Avoid jargon;
- Be comprehensible to all staff and parents;
- Promote effective planning by teachers;
- Help pupils understand what progress they are making;
- Link assessments of the progress of all pupils, including those with SEN, to the school;
- Result in sound preparation and action by the staff, and the achievement of specific learning goals for the pupil.

(OFSTED 1999c: 3. para. 11)

A good IEP will:
- Be brief and action based;
- Indicate the pupil's current levels of achievement;
- Identify the nature, extent and specific areas of a pupil's learning difficulty;
- Specify the learning programme and set specific relevant targets to be achieved, against criteria which acknowledge success, and represent achievable goals;
- Specify any other additional support or resources;
- Indicate how parents or carers will be involved, and what support or encouragement is being provided;
- Include where appropriate, contributions from the pupil and their views on their learning needs;
- Set clear monitoring and recording arrangements with dates;
- Set dates for the next review with parents and teachers.

DFEE (1997a: part 2, 2.3)

IEPs should:
- Identify success criteria which are readily achievable and can be assessed quickly and be understood by parents, pupils and teachers;
- Include how the outcome is assessed and how progression is measured;
- Be clear and easy to use as working documents;
- Tie in with established routines and procedures within the school;
- Be linked with existing planning and assessment at all levels.

(DFEE 1997a: part 2, 2.4)

> As part of their responsibilities under the Code, implement and keep records on individual education plans (IEPs) for pupils at Stage 2 of the Code and above.
>
> (QTS Standards; DfEE 1998a: Annex A: B.4.l)

Where a group of pupils in a class or year group share similar learning difficulties in relation to literacy and numeracy, a Group EDP can be implemented. The Group EDP should focus on precise learning targets which all children in the group can achieve. However, the assessment of whether targets have been achieved must be made on an individual basis.

Differentiated performance criteria for pupils with learning difficulties

- 1998, original descriptions of attainment for pupils leading up to National Curriculum level 1 (P1–P8), and with NC levels 1 and 2 (1C, 1B, 1A, 2C, 2B, 2A) in language and literacy and mathematics, and P1 to P15 in Personal and Social Development.
- Revised P scales (2001) embedded across all subjects of the National Curriculum, including RE, PSHE and Citizenship. Designed for pupils working below NC level 1. P scales adopt smaller steps for measuring pupils' attainment (P1(a), P1(b), P2(a), P2(b), P3(a), P3(b), P4, P5, P6, P7, P8).
- Measure progress for pupils of compulsory school age, with learning difficulties.
- Useful when making summative assessments at the end of an academic year, or at the end of a Key Stage.
- Apply the 'best fit' judgement in relation to pupil attainment.
- The differentiated criteria should be stated on the pupil's IEP, just as National Curriculum levels should.
- The differentiated descriptions are useful for setting specific targets on an IEP in the aspects of language and literacy, mathematics and personal and social development.

(For further information refer to DfEE (1998c: Part 2).)

IEP targets

The class or subject teacher's involvement in drawing up an IEP Action Plan is important in relation to what a pupil with SEN is expected to learn within a set timescale.

Targets for IEPs come from assessment of pupils' progress within the curriculum and from individual profiles of strengths and weaknesses.

Effective target setting requires the teacher to understand how children learn, and to know the effect of different teaching approaches on pupil progress.

Successful IEP targets should have an impact on pupil learning in the wider curriculum context.

The teacher needs to evaluate the pupil's progress in achieving their IEP targets, in relation to the attainment level they started from.

> ... makes an appropriate contribution to the preparation, implementation, monitoring and review of IEPs.
> (NQT Induction Standards; DfEE 1999a: Annex A: 2d)

Guidance on IEP/PSP target setting

- Record what the pupil's primary learning or behaviour problem is.
- Break down what the pupil is expected to learn into smaller parts.
- Convert the smaller parts into specific targets.
- Set no more than three or four targets per term.
- Write the targets in order of priority, as positive, desirable, expected outcomes.
- Ensure that targets are **SMART** (specific, measurable, achievable, relevant and time-related).
- Targets should promote success, encourage a positive attitude to work, be motivating, challenging, interesting and linked to the curriculum.
- Try to involve parents and the pupil in the target-setting process.
- Ensure that the pupil knows what their targets are – and have them written down in their exercise books or personal journal.

Examples of SMART Targets for IEPs

Language and literacy
- Will be able to spell the key words in ____ with 80 per cent accuracy.
- Will be able to retell the main events in a story.
- Will write their full name and address correctly.
- Will use capital letters and full stops correctly when writing sentences.
- Will complete four lines of neat cursive writing in one day.

Mathematics
- Will be able to count forwards and backwards from 1 to 20.
- Will give the number of hundreds, tens and units in any three-digit figure.
- Will be able to recall and recite correctly the 9 times table.
- Will be able to give the correct change from values up to £1.
- Will know how many seconds are in a minute and how many minutes are in an hour.

Behaviour
- Will remain on task for 10 minutes at a time in a lesson.
- Will put up his hand to ask a question.
- Will arrive at lessons on time.
- Will put all equipment away after use, in the correct place.
- Will listen attentively to instructions.

IEP Action Plan

Pupil name: _____ Date of birth: _____

Stage: _____ Nature of need: ☐ learning ☐ behaviour   Action Plan No.: _____

Date IEP began: _____ Teacher: _____

Subject/theme: _____

Targets: (Cross-curriculum and subject access targets. What you expect the pupil to know, understand and be able to do).

	Achieved	Working towards	Not achieved
1. _____	☐	☐	☐
2. _____	☐	☐	☐
3. _____	☐	☐	☐

Teaching/support arrangements

Total class/group size: _____ Ability of group: _____

In-class support provided: ☐ Yes ☐ No   Frequency of in-class support: _____

How will the targets be met? (Please specify: differentiated curriculum materials used, teaching approaches adopted, alternative methods of recording for pupil output)

_____

_____

_____

_____

Homework record: ☐ Excellent   ☐ Good   ☐ Satisfactory   ☐ Poor

Pupil progress grades: (Grades A to E)

Effort: _____ Attainment: _____ Attitude: _____ Behaviour: _____

NC/'P' Level: _____ No. of points/merits awarded: _____

Review of progress (Comment on pupil progress, attainment, attitude, motivation and behaviour, if appropriate. Which targets have been met?):

_____

_____

_____

Recommended future action (future targets for the next term):

_____

_____

_____

Subject/class teacher signature: _____ Date: _____

SENCO/HOD signature: _____ Date: _____

Review date: _____

Pastoral Support Programmes

Pastoral Support Programmes (PSPs) were introduced by the DfEE in its guidance on social inclusion. The seven groups of pupils identified as being at high risk of exclusion are: looked-after children; children with SEN; ethnic minority children; travellers; young carers; children from families under stress; pregnant schoolgirls and teenage mothers.

> Pupils who do not respond to school actions to combat disaffection may be at serious risk of permanent exclusion or criminal activity, and may need a longer term intervention to keep them from dropping out of school altogether. Teachers should actively identify such young people. Each one will need a Pastoral Support Programme worked up with external services.   (DfEE 1999d: 5)

What is a PSP?

- A PSP is a school intervention similar to an IEP, to help pupils manage their behaviour.
- The PSP sets short-term behaviour targets for pupils to achieve via fortnightly tasks.
- It outlines the additional support and provision needed to enable the pupil to achieve their targets.
- Examples of additional strategies to support behaviour targets include: study support; increased in-class support; pastoral mentoring and counselling; college link courses or work placements; and a literacy programme to improve basic skills.
- The PSP should indicate the rewards and sanctions allotted to the pupil.
- Pupils should know what their PSP targets are and refer to them in each lesson.
- Parents are informed of the progress the pupil makes on PSP.
- A PSP is reviewed after eight weeks.
- The PSP is planned for 16 weeks, but it can be renewed for a further 16 weeks or extended period, as necessary.
- The school informs the LEA of pupils who have a PSP.
- Other external support agencies are involved in the PSP: EP, Education Welfare Officer (EWO), Behaviour Support Service, Social Services.

Irrespective of whether your school has a short or full OFSTED inspection, the focus will be on the quality and impact of teaching in relation to pupil progress, attainment and attitudes, across the full ability range.

OFSTED Inspections and SEN

Teacher checklist for OFSTED

Be prepared! Inspectors will focus on:

- the impact on learning in relation to pupils on the SEN Register
- finding out what pupils have learnt in a lesson, by asking questions, and listening to pupils' answers to teacher questions
- examining pupils' written work and teacher comments on marked work

and finding out whether:

- teacher planning indicates that work is matched to pupils' individual needs
- the planning facilitates successful liaison between teacher, support staff and the SENCO
- the teachers use assessment data and SEN information to set appropriate challenging targets for SEN pupils
- IEP targets are clear and practical for class/subject teachers to implement when in-class support is not available
- SEN pupils make sufficient progress towards the targets set in IEPs
- in-class support is effective, and if it encourages SEN pupil independence
- SEN pupils transfer literacy and numeracy knowledge across the curriculum
- homework is appropriately differentiated to meet individual needs
- the curriculum is delivered in a lively, informative, well structured way
- pupil groupings are appropriate to promote high standards
- teachers' questions challenge pupils' thinking
- purposeful practical activities are set by the teacher to extend pupils' learning
- classroom organisation fosters effective teacher/pupil interaction
- a range of stimulating curriculum resources from different cultures is used
- clear lesson objectives are set, so the pupils know what they are doing, and why they are doing it
- new learning builds on previous knowledge.

OFSTED Inspections and Inclusion

Gifted and talented pupils

The OFSTED inspectors will check:

- how the teacher makes use of identification data to make appropriate provision in lessons
- that work provided is intellectually challenging, and does not result in underachievement
- that teaching is adapted and adjusted to take account of pupils' rapid learning development
- that appropriate subject/pastoral mentoring is provided, and the teacher liaises with the mentor
- how the teacher utilises additional resources, projects and master classes to support the most able pupils.

EAL pupils

The OFSTED inspectors will check that:

- the teachers' lesson planning, teaching methods and curriculum delivery take account of the language and learning needs of EAL pupils
- there is opportunity for supported speaking and listening activities
- effective models of spoken and written English are provided
- the teacher is clear about how the pupil's first language can support the learning of English
- appropriate, high quality, culturally relevant resources and visual aids are used
- bilingual assistants are deployed effectively in class, and that withdrawal teaching is kept to a minimum
- English competency is checked against National Curriculum levels.

EBD pupils

The OFSTED inspectors will check that:

- the working atmosphere in the classroom is purposeful, and that proper work habits are established
- the teacher exercises authority clearly and fairly
- the pupil's attention is held, concentration is good and they are actively involved in learning
- pupil grouping is organised appropriately in relation to behaviour management
- teacher intervention supports and controls pupils
- mutual respect exists between teacher and pupil
- the teacher expects pupils to behave in a mature manner
- pupil self-discipline is emphasised.

Part 4

Productive Partnerships

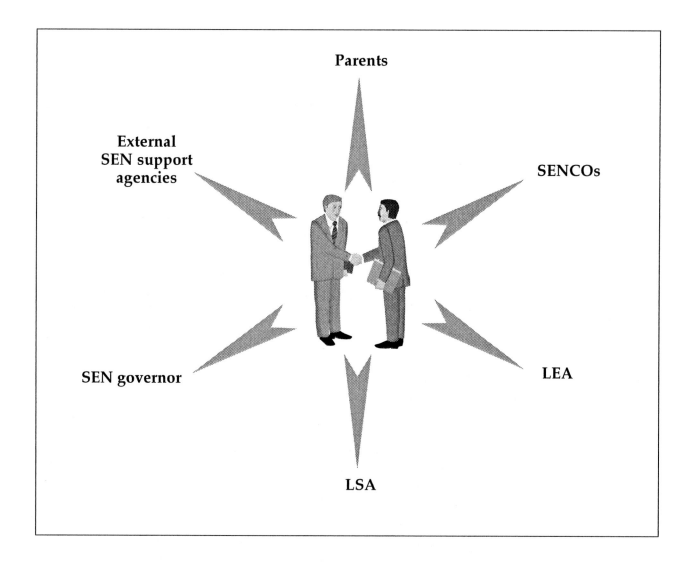

SENCOs

> SENCOs will have an important role in providing specialist support to new teachers during their first year.
>
> (DfEE 1997b: 6:6)

> SENCOs . . . provide support and training to trainee and newly qualified teachers in relation to the standards for the award of Qualified Teacher Status, Career Entry Profile and Standards for induction.   (TTA 1998: 5C.v)

Key areas of responsibility for the SENCO

- Day-to-day operation of the school's SEN policy.
- Liaising with and advising fellow teachers in securing high quality teaching for SEN pupils.
- Coordinating provision for children with SEN.
- Maintaining the school's SEN Register and overseeing the records of all SEN pupils.
- Liaising with parents of SEN children.
- Contributing to the in-service training of staff, and disseminating examples of good SEN practice.
- Liaising with external agencies.
- Effective use of resources to bring about improved standards of achievement for all pupils.
- Ensuring staff follow the SEN Code of Practice procedures.

SENCO support to NQTs/ITT students

- Meeting with the SENCO to discuss SEN school policy, practice and inclusion.
- Observation of the SENCO teaching, and dissemination of practical strategies in relation to children's learning styles.
- Contribution of SENCO to the Induction programme in aspects of: IEPs and target setting, pupil behaviour management, differentiation to enhance curriculum access and identification of SEN.
- Direct NQTs/ITT students to SEN in-service education and training (INSET), in-house, and regionally/nationally.
- Deploy additional LSA in-class support to NQT lessons.
- Provide guidance to NQT on how best to manage and utilise additional support.
- Submit comments for the NQT Induction Summative Assessment Form in relation to SEN.
- Arrange visits for NQTs to local special schools, or another phase of school, in order to view SEN practice.

Additional in-class support for SEN pupils can be provided by: parent volunteers, classroom assistants, special support assistants, nursery nurses or teachers. Each of these individuals will bring a varying degree of SEN expertise, knowledge and skills into the classroom.

Working with LSAs

> ... the value of a classroom assistant lies not only in the ability of the assistant but in that of the teacher to use such help to the full. (Woolf & Bassett 1988: 63)

The term Learning Support Assistant (LSA) refers to any adult, other than a qualified teacher, who provides in-class support to SEN children with statements, or who require specialist intervention.

Whether you are an NQT or an ITT student teaching a class, you will have the responsibility for managing and deploying additional in-class support effectively.

> When classroom assistants are well used and managed their contribution is associated with higher quality teaching. (OFSTED 1995: para. 88: 43)

The aim of in-class support is for the assistant to use a range of intervention and support strategies during the teaching delivery, in order to:

- facilitate maximum curriculum access for SEN children
- encourage the child to remain on task and be more focused
- reduce the incidence of off-task behaviour, or disruption
- foster greater pupil independence
- increase the child's self-esteem and confidence
- raise SEN pupil attainment
- ensure maximum pupil participation.

Having LSAs in the classroom with SEN children is essential in making inclusion work. Too much withdrawal from the mainstream classroom is likely to reduce the child's participation in whole-class learning experiences and activities, and limit their curriculum entitlement opportunities.

> ... manage, with support from an experienced specialist teacher if necessary, the work of parents and other adults in the classroom to enhance learning opportunities for pupils. (QTS Standards; DfEE 1998a: Annex A: B.5.h)

Working collaboratively with LSAs

The Green Paper *Excellence for All Children. Meeting Special Educational Needs* states:

> ... It is the responsibility of all teachers and support staff in a school
>
> • To be aware of the school's responsibilities for children with SEN;
> • To have regard to the guidance of the Code of Practice;
> • To apply that guidance effectively in assessing and teaching children with SEN, and
> • To work together in the classroom to raise standards for all pupils. (DfEE 1997b: 6:2)

How teachers can support the LSA

- Be clear about the role of the LSA – obtain a copy of their job description.
- When planning, incorporate the LSA role within your teaching approaches.
- Clarify the role you want the LSA to adopt at particular stages in the lesson.
- Inform the LSA about the aims, objectives, content, strategies and intended outcomes of the lesson.
- Make your expectations for SEN pupil learning outcomes clear to the LSA.
- Provide regular opportunities for joint planning meetings and discussion.
- Share the responsibility for differentiating curriculum materials and provide clear guidance to the LSA about what you require.
- Don't make unrealistic requests or demands of the LSA.
- Give the LSA guidance about implementing any individual or small group programmes that you have planned.
- Provide, well in advance, any schemes of work, syllabuses, and text books to the LSA in order to secure their curriculum knowledge.
- Encourage the LSA to use their own initiative, talents, expertise, and to introduce any relevant additional materials.
- Provide opportunities for the LSA to work with more able pupils.
- Deploy the LSA to circulate the classroom and to support individual children discreetly.
- Establish agreed procedures with the LSA regarding pupil discipline, classroom rules, routines and procedures.
- Ensure you establish clear ground rules regarding confidentiality with the LSA.
- Include the LSA in any relevant subject/whole-school INSET.
- Share feedback about SEN pupil progress and attainment with the LSA.
- Provide constructive feedback to the LSA about the value and contribution of their support work within your classroom.

> Where applicable deploys support staff and other adults
> effectively in the classroom, involving them, where appropri-
> ate, in the planning and management of pupils' learning.
> (NQT Induction Standards; DfEE 1999a: Annex A: 2:h)

The role of the LSA in the primary school

- Help to plan children's work in conjunction with the class teacher.
- Prepare and maintain curriculum materials.
- Contribute ideas and suggestions based on their personal knowledge, interests and experience.
- Reinforce and consolidate children's learning.
- Organise the classroom and the resources for group work.
- Regularly discuss, with the teacher, routine activities and new topics to be introduced.
- Support and oversee group activities, under teacher supervision, and check that they run smoothly.
- Address pupil's individual needs. Help to support reading, spelling, handwriting, communication, mathematics and behaviour.
- Implement a child's IEP.
- Assist the teacher in implementing the literacy hour and daily mathematics lesson.
- Mount and display children's work.
- Supervise children in any structured outdoor play activities, or during educational visits.
- Keep records of children's effort and progress.
- Report children's achievements to the teacher.
- Contribute to reviews on pupil progress.
- Assist children in using the computer.
- Supervise pupils using any equipment.
- Explain and repeat instructions.
- Help pupils to stay on task and concentrate.
- Assist pupils with basic physical needs, e.g. toileting, dressing.
- Attend any relevant INSET.
- Liaise with SEN pupils' parents, where appropriate.
- Implement any specialist programmes set by external agencies, for speech and language or behaviour management.

The role of the LSA in the secondary school

- Clarifying and explaining instructions, questions, tasks.
- Keeping pupils on task.
- Overseeing the safe use of equipment.
- Assisting with the recording of homework, class work.
- Reading extracts from text or unfamiliar words.
- Assisting pupils in organising and presenting their work.
- Monitoring pupil behaviour.
- Differentiating curriculum materials, tasks, and homework.
- Encouraging and praising SEN pupils for their effort, in order to raise their self-esteem and confidence.
- Meeting regularly with the teacher to discuss pupil progress in meeting IEP targets.
- Maintaining confidentiality regarding pupils' personal details and classroom practice.
- Reinforcing learning and key concepts.
- Helping pupils with proof reading and redrafting their work.
- Helping to develop pupils' study skills.
- Suggesting ideas and practical strategies to enable pupils to tackle teaching tasks more easily
- Providing basic writing equipment to SEN pupils.
- Helping pupils to revise for tests and examinations.
- Encouraging pupils to participate in class discussion and oral work.
- Developing positive relationships of trust with pupils, and the teacher.
- Attending relevant INSET.
- Supervising pupils using the computer or the school library.
- Maintaining records of in-class support.
- Contributing information about pupil progress, performance and attainment.
- Attending SEN pupils' review meetings, where appropriate.

Clear communication and mutual respect promote positive relationships between teachers and parents. Both teachers and parents share a common ground in both having the best interests of the child at heart. Some parents may feel guilty and blame themselves because their child appears 'different' to other children and has SEN. These parents experience additional pressures and may be sensitive or reactionary to teachers' comments about their child's lack of progress or behaviour.

There are largely two types of parents:

1. **Articulate over-anxious parents** who readily communicate their concerns about their child's lack of progress, and hold high expectations.
2. **Those lacking in confidence** who rarely attend meetings at school, and who appear to be unconcerned about their child's lack of progress or poor behaviour.

The SEN Code of Practice states:

> Children's progress will be diminished if their parents are not seen as partners in the educational process with unique knowledge and information to impart . . .   (DfE 1994a: para. 2.28)

It is also useful to try to put yourself in the parents' position, and try to view the situation from their perspective. Imagine how it must feel to contend with an extremely challenging child at home.

Remember that 87 per cent of a child's time during a school year is spent at home with parents.

> The knowledge, views and experience of parents are vital. Effective assessment and provision will be secured where there is the greatest possible degree of partnership between parents and their children and school, LEA and other agencies.
>
> (DfE 1994a: para. 1.2)

Remember, the insights and opinions of parents about their children are just as valid as those of teachers and other professionals.

> Recognise that learning takes place inside and outside the school context, and understand the need to liaise effectively with parents and other carers . . .
>
> (QTS Standards; DfEE 1998a: Annex A: D.g)

Working in Partnership with Parents of SEN Pupils

Meeting with Parents

Key characteristics

Parents:
- have first-hand relevant experience and information about their child
- genuinely want to do what is best for their child
- desire to cooperate with the school
- will be willing to help their child if they can see real benefits in doing so
- can make valuable contributions to their child's education
- are the primary educators of their child
- may feel insecure and believe that they are asking for, or expecting too much
- may be critical and angry about events in school
- may be unwilling to accept that their child has SEN
- may be unable to accept the teacher's point of view.

Practical solutions

- Prepare in advance for the meeting and have evidence of the child's capabilities, i.e. examples of work, starting with strengths.
- Explain to the parents what you have done to help the child.
- Describe in simple terms, without using jargon, the nature of any difficulties that the child has experienced.
- Ask the parents if they know of any factors that could be causing their child to experience difficulties.
- Give the parents a chance to say how they think their child could be helped more.
- Suggest strategies that you and the parents could adopt, to support the child in overcoming the problem.
- Listen attentively to parents, show interest, and give them the opportunity to 'open-up' and air their concerns.
- Ask parents to clarify any issues.
- Write parental concerns down, clarify these with the parent, and agree a plan of action, ensuring parental involvement.
- Involve the parents in setting clear targets for their child's IEP.
- Encourage parents to support their child's learning at home.
- If the meeting runs past the available time, arrange another meeting.
- Telephone parents who don't attend meetings, and give them a verbal report about their child's achievements, and areas for further development.

Top ten tips on writing reports to parents

- Don't waffle, don't make subjective comments, or use technical jargon: just get straight to the point.
- Ensure that the report comments are informative.
- Be positive about the outcomes achieved by the child.
- Specify clearly which targets the child has met, and how they have met these successfully.
- Give the current level of attainment, and indicate clearly how the child has progressed or regressed.
- Indicate how you are going to address any unmet targets, or difficulties that the child is still experiencing.
- Don't ever write any report comment that you cannot justify or support with evidence.
- Avoid using comment banks. These can be impersonal. Parents may compare their child's report with that of others, and the use of standard phrases may not instil parental confidence.
- Where appropriate, award a pupil with SEN a higher effort grade to raise their self-esteem, and to compensate for a lower attainment grade.
- Ensure that your reports are grammatically accurate and contain no spelling mistakes.

> ... liaises effectively with pupils' parents/carers through informative oral and written reports on pupils' progress and achievements, discussing appropriate targets, and encouraging them to support their children's learning, behaviour and progress.   (Induction Standards; DfEE 1999a: Annex A:2g)

The Role of the SEN Governor

> ... governors have statutory responsibilities to publish information in their annual report about the school's SEN policy and about the school's admission arrangements for pupils with disabilities, including how the school will help some pupils gain access ...
>
> Governors should therefore be actively involved in developing, supporting and reviewing the school's policy on SEN in consultation with the headteacher and SENCO.
>
> (DfEE 1997b: 6.18)

The entire governing body is legally responsible for SEN policy and practice within the school. The school will also nominate a governor for SEN. What does the SEN Governor do?

The role of the SEN Governor

The SEN Governor should:

- keep abreast of SEN legislation, and local SEN developments
- liaise with the SENCO and learning support staff termly to discuss SEN issues, curriculum provision, resourcing and staffing
- know the numbers of SEN children on the SEN Register at various stages
- visit classrooms by arrangement with the head teacher/SENCO to observe teaching, monitor SEN resources, and understand pupils' diversity
- monitor SEN expenditure and know how much of the school's budget is allocated to special needs
- communicate and meet with parents of SEN pupils
- liaise and consult with other governors, e.g. literacy and numeracy governor
- join any school or LEA SEN working groups
- attend LEA SEN Governor training sessions, as well as school-based INSET
- make representations to the LEA on behalf of the governing body in relation to SEN resourcing and provision
- be involved in the appointment of the school's SENCO.

The Educational Psychologist

The EP will become involved with SEN pupils at School Action Plus and above. They offer advice to teachers, support staff and parents on the most appropriate provision and strategies to adopt in order to address the child's learning and behavioural difficulties. They also undertake assessments for the statementing process. The EP may observe a pupil with SEN in lessons, to inform their decision-making. The SENCO is the link person who will make referrals to the EP service on your behalf. As the class, form or subject teacher, you may be asked to provide evidence of the child's learning or behavioural difficulties to the EP. The EP will also advise on appropriate IEP target setting for SEN pupils.

The Education Welfare Officer

The EWO monitors pupils in your form or class who have poor records of attendance, or who truant frequently. They work closely with the psychological service and the social services, if they are involved with the child. The EWO liases with the pastoral staff, or the senior management team in the primary school. The EWO will also support and advise parents, and pay home visits as necessary. They may also work with individual school-refusers by counselling them, and building up their self-esteem.

Peripatetic learning support teacher

The peripatetic learning support teacher supports statemented pupils and those at School Action Plus. They focus attention on improving basic literacy and numeracy skills. The learning support teacher may withdraw pupils for individual or small group tuition following a specialist programme. Ideally, it is preferable that they remain in class with the SEN pupil(s) in order to benefit from full curriculum access.

The learning support teacher can give advice to subject/class teachers about appropriate curriculum differentiation, as well as provide additional learning resources. They can also provide guidance on IEP target setting and attend SEN pupils' review meetings.

Peripatetic EBD outreach teacher

These teachers target EBD pupils with statements, as well as those at School Action Plus. They work with pupils who pose extremely challenging behaviour problems in mainstream. They also support children in being reintegrated back into mainstream schools from special EBD schools or PRUs. The teacher may undertake short-term or long-term individual intervention work with pupils. They may implement a behaviour management programme, and work on building up the child's self-esteem. They advise teachers on behaviour strategies to employ in the classroom, as well as about curriculum differentiation. Help and guidance can also be given about IEP/PSP target setting for behaviour.

61

Peripatetic sensory support services

Teachers for hearing impaired and visually impaired children focus on enabling these pupils to access the National Curriculum in mainstream schools. They make an assessment of the pupil's learning needs and advise on the care and provision of hearing and visual aids, illumination levels, curriculum adaptations, signing for the deaf and dumb, classroom acoustics and school building access. INSET can be provided on the appropriate teaching and support strategies to employ for pupils with sensory impairments. Special Support Assistants may also work under the direction of sensory support teachers, and assist in the modification of curriculum materials.

Careers Officer

The Careers Officer plays an important part in statemented pupils' transitional reviews and annual statement reviews, from Year 9 onwards. The Careers Officer will interview the statemented pupil and administer an individual careers audit to discover the pupil's strengths, interests and areas of work they would be interested in. The Careers Officer will devise an individual careers action plan for the pupil, which is reviewed annually, in negotiation with the pupil, their parents and the SENCO or head of year. The Careers Officer will also attend annual review meetings.

The following external support agencies are under the direction of the health service.

Speech and language therapist

The speech and language therapist (SLT) will assess, work with and support individual children who have significant difficulties with their use and understanding of language. These pupils may be on the autistic spectrum disorder continuum, have a physical speech impairment or merely a language delay. The SLT can provide advice to teachers and support assistants on how best to make the curriculum accessible. They can also undertake individual direct teaching using a language programme. In addition, they can oversee the work of an LSA implementing a language programme with a SEN pupil. The SLT can advise on appropriate IEP target setting in relation to speech and language, and also provide INSET to schools on request.

Paediatric occupational therapist

The occupational therapist provides information, advice, training and equipment about improving a child's physical access to activities in school and at home.

They may implement programmes designed to develop a child's fine motor coordination, or address their perceptual difficulties. The occupational therapist works with children who have physical disabilities, or coordination difficulties such as dyspraxia.

The Assistant Education Officer

The AEO works under the direction of the Education Officer for SEN. Their role is largely linked to the statementing process, statutory assessment, and preparing documentation in support of the LEA at SENT appeals. They offer the SENCO advice and guidance regarding appropriate SEN provision to meet the legal requirements of statements of SEN. The AEO advises parents during statutory assessment. They also attend annual statement reviews in school, where appropriate.

Parent Partnership Officer

The PPO's main role is to work in partnership with parents, and provide impartial advice and guidance in relation to any concerns parents may have regarding the SEN of their child. The PPO may help parents complete forms in connection with the statementing process or the SENT appeals procedure. They conciliate, mediate and negotiate between parents and the LEA in order to reach an agreement and resolve any disputes or misunderstandings over SEN issues.

The PPO may also produce publicity material for parents and schools, which explains their role.

The General Adviser for SEN

The LEA SEN Adviser will:

- provide training for senior managers, teachers and SEN Governors on aspects of SEN
- participate in SEN training for NQTs within the Induction programme
- provide individual SEN advice, guidance and support to schools
- prepare SENCOs for their supporting role with NQTs and ITT students
- disseminate good SEN practice throughout the LEA
- direct teachers to practical SEN resources and further information
- monitor SEN policy and practice in schools
- monitor the attainment of SEN pupils.

The Role of the LEA

The General Adviser responsible for NQTS

The designated General Adviser represents the appropriate body (LEA). Their role entails:

- responsibility for training NQTs and Induction Tutors
- supervising and overseeing the NQT induction process
- deciding in conjunction with the head teacher, whether the NQT has successfully met the QTS/NQT Induction Standards
- dealing with any school enquiries regarding NQT induction
- keeping a database of all NQTs employed in the LEA
- collecting NQT summative assessment forms at the end of each term
- retaining NQT assessment reports until the General Teaching Council confirms that the NQT has moved from provisional to full registration, or has been removed from the register, at the end of the induction year
- ensuring they are aware of the reasons why an NQT's summative assessment report has not been submitted or signed
- contacting other LEAs where NQTs are part-time and working in more than one school in one authority
- liaising with professional organisations and personnel at the LEA, when difficulties arise between the NQT and the school, or the NQT is likely to fail the induction year
- maintaining contact with the TTA/DfEE regarding any NQT induction issues
- evaluating the effectiveness of the NQT and Induction Tutor training programme
- monitoring a 10 per cent sample of NQTs in the LEA, to ensure consistent application of QTS/NQT Induction Standards.

Appendix

Useful Information

The Fulton Special Education Digest, Ann Worthington.
The Special Education Handbook, Michael Farrell.

Core concerns

Changing Behaviour. Teaching Children with Emotional and Behavioural Difficulties in Primary and Secondary Classrooms, Sylvia McNamara and Gill Moreton.
Managing Behaviour in Classrooms, John Visser.
Attention Deficit/Hyperactivity Disorder. A Practical Guide for Teachers, Paul Cooper and Katherine Ideus.
Meeting the Needs of Children with Autistic Spectrum Disorders. Rita Jordan and Glenys Jones
Asperger Syndrome: A Practical Guide for Teachers. Val Cumine, Julia Leach and Gill Stevenson.
Teaching Reading and Spelling to Dyslexic Children: Getting to Grips with Words. Margaret Walton.
Maths for the Dyslexic: A Practical Guide. Anne Henderson.
Dyspraxia: A Guide for Teachers and Parents. Kate Ripley, Bob Dames and Jenny Barrett.
Able Children in Ordinary Schools. Deborah Eyre.
Assessing the Needs of Bilingual Pupils: Living in Two Languages. Deryn Hall.

Legal requirements

Implementing the Code of Practice for Children with Special Educational Needs: A Practical Guide. Ahmad F. Ramjhun.
The SENCO Handbook: Working within A Whole School Approach. Elizabeth Cowne.
At the Crossroads: Special Educational Needs and Teacher Education. John Dwyfor Davies.
New Labour's Policies for Schools. Raising the Standard? Jim Docking.

Planning progress

Implementing the Literacy Hour for Pupils with Learning Difficulties. Ann Berger, Jean Henderson and Denise Morris.
Implementing the National Numeracy Strategy For Pupils with Learning Difficulties: Access to The Daily Mathematics Lesson. Ann Berger, Denise Morris and Jane Portman.

Links with other David Fulton Publications: A Selection

Understanding Differentiation: A Teacher's Guide. Sylvia McNamara and Gill Moreton.

IEPs – Implementing Effective Practice. Janet Tod, Frances Castle and Mike Blamires.

Productive partnerships

Effective In-Class Support: The Management of Support Staff in Mainstream and Special Schools. Stephanie Lorenz.

Working with Parents as Partners in Special Educational Needs. Eileen Gascoigne.

Support Services and the Curriculum: A Practical Guide to Collaboration. Penny Lacey and Jeannette Lomas.

Managing Special Needs in Mainstream Schools: The Role of the SENCO. John Dwyfor Davies, Philip Garner and John Lee.

Key Addresses

Government departments/official agencies

Advisory Centre for Education
(ACE)
1b Aberdeen Studios
22 Highbury Grove
London N5 2DQ
Tel: (020) 7354 8318

Basic Skills Agency
Commonwealth House
1–19 New Oxford Street
London WC1A 1NU
Tel: (020) 7405 4017

DFEE Publications Centre
PO Box 5050
Sherwood Park
Annesley
Nottingham NG15 0DJ
Tel: 0845 602 2260

OFSTED Publication Centre
PO Box 6927
London E3 3NZ
Tel: (020) 7510 0180

QCA Publications
PO Box 99
Sudbury
Suffolk CO10 2SN
Tel: 01787 884444

Special Educational Needs Tribunal
7th Floor
Windsor House
50 Victoria Street
London SW1H 0NW
Tel: (020) 7925 6925

Teacher Training Agency
Publications Unit
Freepost ANG2037
Chelmsford
Essex CM1 1ZY
Tel: 0845 606 0323

Agencies for special educational needs

ADD/ADHD Family Support
Group
1a High Street
Dilton Marsh
Westbury
Wilts BA13 4DL
Tel: 01373 826 045

British Dyslexia Association
98 London Road
Reading
Berkshire RG1 5AU
Tel: 0118 966 8271

British Educational Communication
   Technology Agency (BECTA)
Milburn Hill Road
Science Park
Coventry CV4 7JJ
Tel: 01203 416 994

Centre for Studies in Inclusive
   Education (CSIE)
1 Redland Close
Elm Lane
Redland
Bristol BS6 6UE
Tel: 0117 923 8450

Dyslexia Institute
133 Gresham Road
Staines
Middlesex TW18 2AJ
Tel: 01784 463851

Dyspraxia Foundation
8 West Alley
Hitchin
Herts SG5 1EG
Tel: 01462 454986

Gifted Children's Information
   Centre (GCIC)
Hampton Grange
21 Hampton Lane
Solihull
West Midlands B91 2QJ
Tel: 0121 705 4547

Granada Learning Ltd - SEMERC
Granada Television
Quay Street
Manchester M60 9EA
Tel: 0161 827 2887

Hyperactive Children's Support
   Group
71 Whyke Lane
Chichester,
West Sussex PO19 2LD
Tel: 01903 725182

National Association for Able
   Children in Education (NACE)
Westminster College
Harcourt Hill
Oxford OX2 9AT
Tel: 01865 245657

National Association for Gifted
   Children (NAGC)
Elder House
Milton Keynes MK9 1LR
Tel: 01908 673677

The National Association for
   Language Development in the
   Curriculum (NALDIC)
South Herts LCSC
Holywell School Site
Tolpits Lane
Watford WD1 8NT

National Association for Special
   Educational Needs (NASEN)
NASEN House
4/5 Amber Business Village
Amber Close
Amington
Tamworth
Staffs B77 4RP
Tel: 01827 311500

National Autistic Society
393 City Road
London EC1V 1NG
Tel: (020) 7833 2299

National Children's Bureau
8 Wakley Street
London EC1V 7QE
Tel: (020) 7843 6000

Network 81
1–7 Woodfield Terrace
Stanstead
Essex CM24 8AJ
Tel: 01279 647415

SENJIT
Institute of Education
University of London
20 Bedford Way
London WC1H 0AL
Tel: (020) 7612 6305

Web Sites for SEN

These links will be provided on the David Fulton Publishers website, www.fultonpublishers.co.uk, so that you can just click on them and be taken straight to the relevant page.

www.mailbase.ac.uk/lists/senco-forum

www.education-quest.com

www.inclusive-technology.com/infosite/snhome.htm

inclusion.uwe.ac.uk/csie/csiehome.htm

www.canterbury.ac.uk/xplanatory/xplan.htm

www.semerc.co.uk

www.becta.org.uk

www.nasen.org.uk

www.ace-ed.org.uk

www.nrich.maths.org-uk/index.html

www.bda-dylexia.org.uk

www.dyslexic.com

library.advanced.org/11799/data/dyspraxia.html

www.mailbase.ac.uk/lists/high-ability/files/boys.html

www.inclusion.uwe.ac.uk

www.inclusion.ngfl.gov.uk

www.ipsea.org.uk

www.vicnet.net.au./vicnet/community/asperger-htm

www.ummed.edu./pub/O/ozbayrak

www.ummed.edu/bkirby/asperger

www.users.globalnet.co.uk/~ebdstudy/index.htm

www.basic-skills.co.uk

www.ngfl.gov.uk/ngfl/index.html

www.dfee.gov.uk/senhome.htm

www.nof.org.uk/educ_frame.htm

www.teach-tta.gov.uk/index.htm

www.coi.gov.uk/coi/depts

www.nfer.ac.uk

www.ofsted.gov.uk

www.qca.org.uk

www.teachingtimes.com

www.teaching-today.com

www.mathsyear2000.org

www.scope.org.uk

www.oneworld.org/autism_uk

www.sense.org.uk

Bibliography

ACE (1997) *Tribunal Toolkit going to the Special Educational Needs Tribunal*. London: ACE.

ACE (1998) *Special Needs: Support for Governors*. London: ACE.

ATL (1998) *Achievement for All*. London: ATL.

Ayers, H. *et al.* (1995) *Perspectives on Behaviour: A Practical Guide to Effective Interventions for Teachers*. London: David Fulton Publishers.

Ayers, H. *et al.* (1996) *Assessing Individual Needs: A Practical Approach*. London: David Fulton Publishers.

Basic Skills Agency (1997) *Developing Literacy: A course for teachers of Key Stage 3 and 4*. London: Basic Skills Agency.

Bell, P. and Best, R. (1986) *Supportive Education*. Oxford: Basil Blackwell.

Beveridge, S. (1996) *Spotlight on Special Educational Needs: Learning Difficulties*. Staffordshire: NASEN.

Centre for Studies in Inclusive Education (CSIE) (1999) *Assessments and Statements: CSIE Summary of Part 4 of the Education Act 1996*. Bristol: CSIE.

Centre for Studies in Inclusive Education (CSIE) (2000) *Index for Inclusion developing learning and participation in schools*. Bristol: CSIE.

Cheminais, R. (1997) 'Can I help?', *Special Children* **103**, 15–19.

Clayton, P (1999) 'It all adds up', *Special Children* **122**, 30–32.

Cooper, P. and Ideus, K. (1996a) 'Attention matters', *Special!* Spring 1996, 43–5.

Cooper, P. and Ideus, K. (1996b) *Attention Deficit/Hyperactivity Disorder: A Practical Guide for Teachers*. London: David Fulton Publishers.

Cornwall, J. and Tod, J. (1999) *Individual Education Plans: Emotional and Behavioural Difficulties*. London: David Fulton Publishers.

Cumine, V. *et al.* (1998) *Asperger Syndrome: A Practical Guide for Teachers*. London: David Fulton Publishers.

Department for Education and Employment (DfEE) (1997a) *The SENCO Guide*. London: DfEE.

Department for Education and Employment (DfEE) (1997b) *Excellence for all Children: Meeting Special Educational Needs*. London: DfEE

Department for Education and Employment (DfEE) (1998a) *Teaching: High Status, High Standards. Requirements for Courses of Initial Teacher Training* (Circular 4/98). London: DfEE.

Department for Education and Employment (DfEE) (1998b) *Meeting Special Educational Needs: A Programme of Action*. London: DfEE.

Department for Education and Employment (DfEE) (1998c) *Supporting the Target Setting Process: Guidance for Effective Target Setting for Pupils with Special Educational Needs*. London: DfEE.

Department for Education and Employment (DfEE) (1999a) *The Induction Period for Newly Qualified Teachers* (Circular 5/99) London: DfEE.

Department for Education and Employment (DfEE) (1999b) *The Special Educational Needs Tribunal Regulations 1999*. London: DfEE.

Department for Education and Employment (DfEE) (1999c) *Achieving Dyslexia Friendly Schools*. London: DfEE/BDA.

Department for Education and Employment (DfEE) (1999d) *Social Inclusion: Pupil Support* (Circular 10/99). London: DfEE.

Department for Education and Employment (DfEE) (1999e) *Social Inclusion: The LSA Role in Pupil Support* (Circular 11/99). London: DfEE.

Department for Education and Employment (DfEE) (1999e) *Excellence in Cities*. London: DfEE.

Department for Education and Employment (DfEE) (1999f) *From Exclusion to Inclusion. A Report of the Disability Rights Task Force on Civil Rights for Disabled People*. London: DfEE.

Department for Education and Employment (DfEE) (1999g) *The National Curriculum: Handbook for Primary Teachers in England*. London: DfEE.

Department for Education and Employment (DfEE) (1999h) *The National Curriculum: Handbook for Secondary Teachers in England*. London: DfEE.

Department of Education (DfE) (1994a) *Code of Practice on Identification and Assessment of Special Educational Needs*. London: DfE.

Department of Education (DfE) (1994b) *Special Educational Needs Tribunal: How to Appeal*. London: DfE.

Department of Education and Science (DES) (1989) *Discipline in Schools: Report of the Committee of Enquiry Chaired by Lord Elton*. London: HMSO.

Department of Education and Science (DES) (1992a) *Parents Charter: Children with Special Needs: A Guide for Parents*. London: DES.

Department of Education and Science (DES) (1992b) *Education Observed: Non-Teaching Staff in Schools: A Review by HMI*. London: HMSO.

Dickinson, C. and Wright, J. (1993) *Differentiation: A Practical Handbook of Classroom Strategies*. Coventry: NCET.

Dyer, C. (1988) 'Which support?: an examination of the term', *Support for Learning* **3**(1), 6–10.

Dyslexia Institute (1999) *Assessment and Provision for Children*. Staines: Dyslexia Institute.

Dyson, A. and Gains, C. (1995a) *Rethinking Special Needs in Mainstream Schools Towards the Year 2000*. London: David Fulton Publishers.

Dyson, A. and Gains, C. (1995b) 'The role of the special needs co-ordinator: Poisoned chalice or crock of gold?', *Support for Learning* **10**(2), 50–56.

Eyre, D. (1995) *School Governors and More Able Children*. London: DfEE.

Eyre, D. (1997a) 'Teaching able pupils' *Support for Learning*, **12**(2), 60-65.

Eyre, D. (1997b) *Able Children in Ordinary Schools*. London: David Fulton Publishers.

Eyre, D. (1998) *Teaching More Able Pupils*. Oxford: NACE.

Farrell, M. (1997) *The Special Education Handbook*. London: David Fulton Publishers.

Farrell, P. *et al.* (1999) *The Management, Role and Training of Learning Support Assistants* (Research Report 161), London: DfEE.

Fletcher, P. (1990) *Differentiating the Secondary Curriculum (No. 10) Teachers Responses to: Behavioural Issues*. Trowbridge: Wiltshire Education Support and Training.

Fogell, J. and Long. R. (1997) *Spotlight on Special Educational Needs: Emotional and Behavioural Difficulties*. Tamworth: NASEN.

Freeman, J. (1998) *Educating the Very Able. Current International Research*. London: OFSTED, The Stationery Office.

George, D. (1992) *The Challenge of the Able Child*. London: David Fulton Publishers.

George, D. (1995) *Gifted Education: Identification and Provision*. London: David Fulton Publishers.

Henderson, A. (1998) *Maths for the Dyslexic*. London: David Fulton Publishers.

Her Majesty's Inspectorate (HMI) (1992) *Education Observed: The Education of Very Able Children in Maintained Schools. A Review by HMI*. London: HMSO.

Hornsby, B. (1995) *Overcoming Dyslexia. A Straightforward Guide for Families and Teachers*. London: Optima.

House of Commons Education and Employment Committee (1999) *Highly Able Children*, (Third Report) Volume 1. London: The Stationery Office.

Hughes, M. (1999) *Closing the Learning Gap*. Stafford: Network Educational Press.

ISCG (1998) *Checklists: Special Educational Needs The Governor's Role*. London: ISCG.

Kent Local Education Authority (1996) *Able Children Handbook*. Tonbridge: Kent LEA.

Lewis, M. and Wray, D. (2000) *Literacy in the Secondary School*. London: David Fulton Publishers.

Lorenz, S. (1999) *Effective In-Class Support: The Management of Support Staff in Mainstream and Special Schools*. London: David Fulton Publishers.

MacDonald, A. *et al.* (1999) *Boys' Achievement, Progress, Motivation and Participation: Issues Raised by the Recent Literature.* Berkshire: NFER.

McKeown, S. (1999) 'Supporting dyslexic learners', *Special Children* **123**, 19–22.

McNamara, S. and Moreton, G. (1998) *Understanding Differentiation A Teachers Guide.* London: David Fulton Publishers.

NAGM (1996) *Special Educational Needs in Mainstream Schools,* NAGM Paper No. 51. Birmingham: NAGM.

NALDIC (1997) *Bilingual Pupils Learning English as an Additional Language: Guidelines for Classroom and School Practice,* Working Paper 1. Watford: NALDIC.

NALDIC (1998a) *Provision in Literacy Hours for Pupils Learning English as an Additional Language.* Watford: NALDIC.

NALDIC (1998b) *Guidelines on Bilingualism,* Working Paper 3. Watford: NALDIC.

NALDIC (1999) *The Distinctiveness of English as an Additional Language a Cross Curriculum Discipline,* Working Paper 5. Watford: NALDIC.

Newton, M. (1998) 'Standards. Numeracy Strategy 3: IEPs', *Special Children* **109**, 1–12.

Office for Standards in Education (OFSTED) (1993) *Exceptionally Able Children.* London: DfE Publications.

Office for Standards in Education (OFSTED) (1995) *Class Size and the Quality of Education.* London: OFSTED.

Office for Standards in Education (OFSTED) (1998a) *Recent Research on the Achievements of Ethnic Minority Pupils.* London: The Stationery Office.

Office for Standards in Education (OFSTED) (1998b) *Educating the Very Able: Current International Research.* London: The Stationery Office.

Office for Standards in Education (OFSTED) (1999a) *Raising the Attainment of Minority Ethnic Pupils: School and LEA responses.* London: OFSTED.

Office for Standards in Education (OFSTED) (1999b) *Pupils with Specific Learning Difficulties in Mainstream Schools. A Survey of the Provision in Mainstream Primary and Secondary Schools for Pupils with a Statement of Special Educational Needs Relating to Specific Learning Difficulties.* London: OFSTED.

Office for Standards in Education (OFSTED) (1999c) *The SEN Code of Practice Three Years on. The Contribution of Individual Education Plans to the Raising of Standards for Pupils with Special Educational Needs.* London: OFSTED.

Office for Standards in Education (OFSTED) (1999d) *Inspecting Schools. Handbook for Inspecting Primary and Nursery Schools.* London: The Stationery Office.

Office for Standards in Education (OFSTED) (1999e) *Inspecting Schools: Handbook for Inspecting Secondary Schools.* London: The Stationery Office.

Pollock, J. (1999) 'In the mind's eye', *Special Children* **122,** 25–7.

Qualifications and Curriculum Authority (QCA) (1999) *Early Learning Goals.* London: QCA.

Qualifications and Curriculum Authority (2000a) *A Language in Common: Assessing English as an Additional Language.* London: QCA.

Qualifications and Curriculum Authority (QCA) (2000b) Assessment Criteria for pupils with emotional and behavioural difficulties. London: QCA.

Ripley, K. *et al.* (1997) *Dyspraxia. A Guide for Teachers and Parents.* London: David Fulton Publishers.

Robertson, F. (1994) *Strategies for Improving Behaviour in the Classroom.* Scunthorpe: Desktop Publishing.

Seach, D. (1998) *Autistic Spectrum Disorder. Positive Approaches for Teaching Children with ASD.* Tamworth: NASEN.

Sebba, J. and Sachdev, D. (1997) *What works in Inclusive Education?* Ilford: Barnardos.

Smith, D. (1996) *Spotlight on Special Educational Needs: Specific Learning Difficulties.* Tamworth: NASEN.

Special Educational Needs Tribunal (SENT) (1995) *Special Educational Needs Tribunal Annual Report 94–95.* London: SENT.

Tod, J. (2000) *Individual Education Plans: Dyslexia.* London: David Fulton Publishers.

Tod, J. *et al.* (1998) *Individual Education Plans Implementing Effective Practice.* London: David Fulton Publishers.

Teacher Training Agency (TTA) (1998) *National Standards for Special Educational Needs Coordinators.* London: TTA.

Teacher Training Agency (TTA) (1999) *National Special Educational Needs Specialist Standards.* London: TTA.

Vahid, B. *et al.* (1998) *500 Tips for Working with Children with Special Needs.* London: Kogan Page.

Watkins, C. (1998) *Managing Classroom Behaviour: A Bit Like Air Traffic Control.* London: ATL.

Woolf, M. and Bassett, S. (1988) 'How classroom assistants respond', *British Journal of Special Education* **15**(2), 62–4.

Index

Printed in the United Kingdom
by Lightning Source UK Ltd.
114372UKS00001B/203-354

9 781853 467073